What readers are saying about 21 Games…

Finally, non-digital games that soothe instead of stress my brain! A.T. Lynne is the master in positive use of that forgotten, magical gift called *Imagination*. I can't think of a better use of my free time during the next three weeks.
—Denis Waitley, Author,
The Psychology of Winning

A.T. has written a practical user's guide for the caretaking of the modern mind. She has completely won over this squeamish self-help book reader. Written with brevity and clarity such that you envision results before playing each memorable game. Even just a dabbling will give your mind a rest.
—Wendy Tremont King
Studiotozzi – Actor/Narrator

With Wisdom distilled in this little volume, A.T. Lynne has profoundly reminded us of the formative power of play. With her *21 Games…* she has convincingly also shown us how our thoughts shape and misshape our mind, and affect both our sense of self and well being. Her games greatly help in the ongoing process of becoming conscious, which ultimately makes individuation achievable. Bravo!   —David B. Leof, M.D.
Distinguished Life Fellow,
American Psychiatric Association
Senior Jungian Training Analyst,
Inter-Regional Society of Jungian Analysts

Brilliant book! I thoroughly enjoyed it and love your processes.
—Rintu Basu
Author, *Persuasion Skills Black Book*
Glasgow, Scotland

What readers are saying about 21 Games...

I read A.T. Lynne's book cover to cover, then went back and worked with each game! Now, I'm integrating *21 Games...* into my daily practice. I like the way it gets my thinking focused and clears the way for progress and growth.

—Mike Clinco
Composer, Jazz Guitarist, Dog Owner

There are lots of ways to calm the anxious, frustrated mind: give up coffee, take up yoga, dope up on prescriptions or buy up the entire self-help section of the bookstore. If you've tried it all and your mind still won't "shut the @#&* up," keep trying. *21 Games...* is a Swiss army knife in the creative person's toolkit for well-being.

—Nancy Shaw
Filmmaker

This book and these "games" are simple, entertaining and thought changing. Spiritual law says that if you can change your thinking, you can change your life. This book has the tools to easily and playfully change your life. Don't believe me, try it for yourself!

—Nancy Radford, RScP

I shared A.T.'s games with my family and they have lead to fun and interesting discussions about how to cope with difficult situations and people. I look forward to giving them all copies of A.T.'s book so they can find the same benefits that I found.

—Morgan Fenner
Berkeley High Rowing Coach

A.T. Lynne's insights into human perception are so positive and illuminating!

—Andre Schjaerve
Artist and Screenwriter

What readers are saying about 21 Games…

Truly, the moment I began reading *21 Games…*, I felt at peace. It was not about "shutting the mind up." It was about breathing life, honoring life's gifts, feeling joyous and at peace. A.T. has channeled a connection with her gift for playfulness to create instant peace and happiness in others.
—Jeni Pfeiffer
Realtor, EcoBroker
Specializing in Green Building

My sister took a writing class from A.T. Lynne and sent me her book for my birthday in April. It has given me many tips for controlling my ADD mind, which I appreciate greatly. Thanks for the peace.
—Allison Green
Evansville, IN

A. T. Lynne's *21 Games for the Mind that Won't Shut the @#&* Up!* smashes down the barricaded door to the panic room in your brain, kicks ass and takes names. Buy it!
Rob Swigart, Author,
*Little America, The Time Trip,
The White Pig* and other novels

I bought the book – looked slender. Got heavier as I carried it… hmmm, got some heavy ideas. Burned through it in one night — walked on air all week. Enjoying its games.
—Delilah, Author,
Excuse Me, Am I Bothering You
Multi-media Artist

Sixty-plus years of dabbling in activity after activity, reinventing myself countless times, listening to the incessant voice of "If only I have this in my life all will be OK" all in the quest of

What readers are saying about 21 Games...

filling the emptiness that was still there when the newness of the objects wore off. What a joy to discover that by redirecting my thoughts and perceptions of the world around me, by playing A.T.'s *21 Games...*, a new guide to true happiness and tranquility is, at last, mine!
—Gordon Christensen
MCO, Retired
NRA Life Member

When feeling uninspired, I use *21 Games...* to boost my creativity. This book is a combination self help manual, puzzle book, and mind expanding guide. Most of all, it's just plain fun. Read it and feel better!
—Stephanie Fuelling
CFO, Harmony Landscapes & Design, Inc.

Man muß noch Chaos in sich haben, um einen tanzenden Stern gebären zu können!

Also sprach Zarathustra
—Friedrich Nietzsche

(Man must have some chaos within, in order to give birth to a dancing star!)

21 Games for The Mind that Won't *Shut the @#&* Up!*

A.T. Lynne

Prime Number Press
Sausalito, California

Published by:
Prime Number Press
Post Office Box 898
Sausalito, CA 94966 U.S.A.
www.primenumberpress.com
info@primenumberpress.com

Copyright © 2010 A.T. Lynne. All rights reserved. No part of this book may be reproduced or transmitted in any form, for public or private use — other than for "fair use" as brief quotations embodied in literature, articles and reviews, without prior written permission from the publisher.

The author of this book does not dispense medical advice nor prescribe the use of any technique as a form of treatment for physical or medical problems, either directly or indirectly. Readers are advised to take the ideas in this book with a grain of salt, as wisdom suggests you do with any other ideas or advice. The intent of the author is only to offer information of a general and playful nature to help you in your quest for emotional, intellectual, financial, mental, social, visceral and spiritual well-being. In the event you use any of this information for yourself or play any of these games with yourself, which is your constitutional right, the author and the publisher assume no responsibility for your actions.

Publisher's Cataloging-in-Publication Data

Lynne, A.T.
21 Games for the Mind that Won't Shut the @#&* Up! / A.T. Lynne
1. Inner Peace   2. Life skills — Success   3. Adult Play   I. Title.

ISBN 978-0-9826666-3-0
LCCN 2010907268

Printed in the United States of America

Design by Pete Masterson, Æonix Publishing Group, www.aeonix.com

1st printing, March 2010, First paperback Edition
2nd printing May, 2010, First paperback Edition
3rd printing January, 2011, First paperback Edition
4th printing September, 2011, First paperback Edition
5th printing February, 2012, Revised paperback Edition

For my wonderful companion

Paul Churchill —

you helped me learn
how to keep the drama on the page
while nurturing playfulness
— and peace —
in our home.

Acknowledgments

Linda Jay Geldens, Skillful Editor par Excellence: the readers of this book and I benefit tremendously from your sharp eye, your devoted attention and your all-around editing mastery;

Pete Masterson, Publishing Guru Extraordinaire: your thorough knowledge of this process and your calm guidance made this book a reality;

Brady Barrows, Hawaii Webmaster Wizard: your technical know-how shifted this book into hyperspace by launching my website a year ago;

Adam Faulconer, Katherine Faulconer and Tracy Faulconer: wherever you are on your cosmic journeys, thank you for everything you contributed to my life while you danced upon the earth;

Margot Rumley and Keith Faulconer: thank you for continuing to boldly live your own wonderful destinies and for your support and encouragement of me in living mine.

Contents

Preface	....	11
Introduction	....	15
Section One	Emergency Rations......................	17
Game #1	Come Home!.............................	18
Game #2	Pick A Color ... Any Color................	21
Game #3	Says Who?	24
Game #4	Master Hypnotist.........................	27
Game #5	Take Five Trance Awakening.............	30
Game #6	I Get To…..............................	34
Game #7	New Thot Box............................	36
Game #8	Up Until Now….........................	40
Game #9	Use Your Drugs	43
Game #10	Aim For The Back Of The Head	48
Section Two	Going Deeper	53
Game #11	Mother Tongue Speaking the Language of Heaven, Hell or Purgatory.........................	54
Game #12	**I'm Outta Here!** Cancelling Your Membership in the Scared S**tless Club	58

Game #13	**About-Face!**	
	Moving *Toward* What You Really Want	...65
Game #14	**Re-spect**	
	"What Else Do I See?"	...70
Game #15	**Play With Yourself—**	
	Producing, Writing and Directing...	
	as well as Starring in Your Life	...74
Game #16	**If I Lived in a Vacuum...**	
	Disengaging from the Joneses	...79
Game #17	**Ridicule**	
	Getting Rid of the Whole Family	...83
Game #18	**I Am Not Sorry!**	
	Never Apologize Again	...87
Game #19	**Off The Hook**	
	Hanging Out with Your Enemies	...94
Game #20	**Paid In Full!**	
	Rescinding the Price for Your Life	
	and Living Debt-free	...100
Game #21	**Skating Away From the Wall**	
	Authoring Your Life	...108

Section Three**** Bonus Game **** 112

Game #22	**Who / What ...**	
	are you saving it for?	...113

Preface

How to gain, how to keep, how to recover happiness is in fact for most men at all times the secret motive of all they do, and of all they are willing to endure.
—William James (1842 – 1910)
American psychologist/philosopher

Imagine for a moment that you recover your happiness, a happiness as great as the greatest days of your childhood. And now, imagine that you recover this happiness simply by playing games. Imagine, then, that you continue playing in such a way that the rest of your long life is truly pleasurable, fruitful and satisfying.

If you can imagine these possibilities, read on.

But, what if you can't really imagine happiness any more. What if you're done with even considering that ridiculous, childish concept. What if all you want is just a few moments, now and then, free of the full-on war in your head.

I invite you, too, to keep reading.

You don't have to believe in happiness to play these games. You don't have to have faith in anything, hope for anything or believe in anything. You can even hold onto the fear-preservers of skepticism and doubt while you begin to play with these new ideas.

However, before we determine whether this book is for you, I must alert those for whom it is not.

This book is not for children. Anyone who still wakes up with unbridled eagerness to leap into the day will only be distracted by this book.

This book is not for the simple. Anyone whose mind has never been troubled by the bedlam of too much adult thinking has no need for these games.

This book is not for people so devoted to their religious faith, their artistic expressions or their inventive imaginations that they go to sleep and wake again into visions of ecstasy, while living in contented communion with their minds. These fortunate ones already occupy those states that players of these games will glimpse.

And, this book isn't for anyone who, in her heart-of-hearts, still believes the answer to unhappiness lies in one more thing that can be bought, one more trip that can be taken, one more guru that can be followed. Her money and time are best invested in that next best thing, not in this book. Yet.

This book is for you only when you've tried everything else. When you've spent every penny you've earned and, then, gone deep in debt still hoping to "make a hand." When you've used every drug you could find, but lack the guts to take enough of it to solve your problems, once and for all. When you've come to the grim conclusion that they're right — you are your own worst enemy.

If any of this relates to you and your life, then we're starting with some things in common. Leaping into life with high expectations, the obligation that I had to take care of myself soon eclipsed the vision that I was here for a grand purpose. After decades of trying to keep my nose to the grindstone, my goal had devolved to getting debt-free before I died. I look back now and wonder, What was I thinking? Was I worried that Mastercard or Visa would trash me in some obituary notice, labeling me a dishonorable debt-payer? I had become more committed to the bottom line of American Express than I was to my own sweet life.

No wonder I wanted to jump off the Golden Gate Bridge! Actually, it's a wonder I didn't.

Driven by the insatiable desire to escape my tormented thinking, I retreated to the remembered state of my eager and untroubled child mind. What I discovered there was a desire to play. As I dared to play, I began to experience moments of respite from the ever-present worry in my adult life. And, over this last decade, I've been developing and playing the games in this book. The very best result has been the re-friending of my own mind.

—Sausalito, California

Introduction

It is said that to make a new behavior into a habit takes about three weeks. It is said by some that an average Lunacy Cycle is also about three weeks. This means, that most of us can hold it together for 21 days before we do something rash, which we soon regret.

Here in your hands you have a few weeks' worth of games to play. Some take a minute while others, played in full, take a week. These games are designed to be played with and by yourself. Each one is a game of non-competitive self-discovery.

Right now, you might not believe that these simple, easy-to-play games can accomplish so much. But suppose for a moment you see yourself smiling with compassion at someone else's angry accusations. Imagine choosing more of what you want and completely enjoying what you choose. Suppose, instead of always having the radio, the TV or your iPod blaring at you 24/7, you're more eager to hear your own ideas, and the quiet hour with yourself is your favorite hour of the day. What if you had the tools to determine the life you live and never again have to do what someone else says? Are these possibilities enough to make a few minutes of playing worth your time?

Lastly, these games are not meant to be slavishly followed. As you experiment and play them, the games will naturally align with what is most fun for you. In time, they will weave into your very own games. In the pattern that is true of children's games, these are merely a means of getting you out into the sunshine, where you will run right into the happy life you were meant to choreograph and live.

Let the Games begin! And, may you find that a little playing has a mighty influence on extending your peace of mind far beyond a few short weeks.

Welcome!

Section One

Emergency Rations

When you're headed to the bridge to jump, headed to a divorce lawyer, or just headed straight to hell in a handbasket, give yourself a minute to play.

The intention of these first ten games is to give you the delicious experience of relief. In the absence of, at least, intermittent relief, the tensions of life can grind down hope, jeopardize health and rob the heart of happiness. Play these games and let the resultant moments of relief surprise you with a renewed sense of possibility.

Game #1

Come Home!

Go placidly amid the noise and the haste, and remember what peace there may be in silence.
—Max Ehrmann (1872-1945)
From "Desiderata"

Have you noticed how much noise flows into your head day and night? First, there's the music, the news, the sports, the conversations, TV, Internet and radio that you choose to listen to. Then add to that the traffic, overheard conversations, boom boxes, public address announcements, and all the other sounds that fill the air around you. Is it any wonder that you sometimes want to shout, "Shut the @#&* up!" Yes, the chaotic noise in your head definitely isn't all in your head.

Now, imagine experiencing one minute of private and personal quiet right where you are. How good would sixty seconds of deep relaxation, anytime you wanted it, feel to your body and mind? Playing the COME HOME! Game gives you that moment of relief, anytime, anywhere.

Step 1. Remove any headphones or Blueteeth from your ears. Turn off any other sound sources under your control.

Step 2. Cup the palms of your open hands gently against your cheeks. Lay your fingers over your eyes and rest your fingertips on your forehead. If you want, you can lean forward, resting your elbows on the surface in front of you. Or, lean back slightly, allowing your elbows to part at a relaxed and easy angle. Close your eyes.

Step 3. Slide your thumbs across your cheekbones until they are over the small flap of skin at the front of your ears. Press your thumbs firmly onto those little flaps, making a comfortably tight seal over the openings of your ears. Close out as much surrounding noise as possible.

Step 4. Let your hands and arms adjust themselves however they need to in order to comfortably hold this position. With your lips gently closed, completely relax your jaw.

Step 5. Begin breathing mindfully. To do this, count your next 10 inhalations and exhalations in this manner: (in) 1-2-3, (out) 2-2-3, (in) 3-2-3, (out) 4-2-3.... As you complete your tenth breath, remain relaxed, and continue resting your face in your hands.

Step 6. Slowly and evenly count backwards from 30 to 1, allowing your body to breathe as it wishes. As you count, notice how much quieter your mind is — no traffic noise, no office noise, no TV or radio, no one else's opinions. Once you have counted back to 1, lower your hands to your lap and open your eyes.

How marvelously freeing it is to realize that what you thought was your own mind's craziness, is actually just an echo of someone else's chatter. Play the COME HOME! Game once or twice a day and refresh your mind in a brand new way.

Bonus Benefit

When you allow it, your body breathes with magnificent ease. Yet, without intending to, you may have developed the habit of holding your breath. Playing the COME HOME! Game will help you renew the natural habit of effortless and easy breathing. This, in turn, will keep your body and mind refreshed all day.

Game #2

Pick A Color
... Any Color

The mind should be allowed some relaxation, that it may return to its work all the better for the rest.
—Seneca (4 BC–65 AD)
Roman philosopher

Driving home from work, do you ever torment yourself with the same problem you were facing at your desk? Does worry occupy you even when you're out for a run? Is your mind still fixated on fears when you're on your long-awaited vacation?

Very often, this mind that's driving you mad simply needs a distraction, a screensaver while the hard drive is still running. Like a fitful child, all your mind asks is to be amused with a simple game when you are driving or doing some other familiar task that doesn't allow you to shut your eyes and play the COME HOME! Game.

The PICK A COLOR...ANY COLOR Game is especially effective for stilling a spinning mind when you are physically moving in the world — in a car, on a bus, walking through an airport terminal or across town.

Step 1. Pick a color. Any color will do. You could pick the most prevalent color in your surroundings, such as green in Florida, or an uncommon one like lavender. However, this game, like every game in this book, is meant to be as easy as possible. So, initially, I suggest that you begin the game with a common color. "Red," for example, if you're driving on a freeway.

Step 2. Say the name of the color out loud. Calmly and effortlessly, simply say the word over and over, "Red, red, red, red...."

Step 3. Making no effort to direct your eyes, notice how they automatically scan the landscape as you continue to say the word. Saying the name of the color is sufficient to prompt your eyes to find it and your mind to notice it.

Step 4. As soon as you see something in that color, let your eyes float onward to the next object. There is no need to consciously name the objects you see. That will only cause your mind to begin thinking and analyzing again. The purpose of this game, remember, is to relax your mind: an effortless mental screensaver while your mind pauses to refresh.

The PICK A COLOR...ANY COLOR Game also happens to be a fine game for enhanced relaxation of your eyes. As you relax the intensity of your thinking, you also ease the constriction of muscles around your eyes. This reduced muscle tension and the sweeping movement of your vision from left to right, up to down, near to far, gives your eyes a gentle and relaxing workout.

Bonus Benefit

When we hold ourselves in the grip of fear and worry, the resultant tension makes thinking of any new options very difficult. In the reprieve from worry and tension that comes with playing the PICK A COLOR…ANY COLOR Game, you'll be pleasantly surprised by the fresh new answers bursting forth from your creative imagination.

Game #3

Says Who?

He who would be useful, strong, and happy, must cease being a passive receptacle for the negative, beggarly, and impure streams of thought.

—James Allen (1864–1912)
As A Man Thinketh

Do you ever feel unhappy or worried because of something you saw on the Internet? Even if that thing happened thousands of miles away or years ago? Have you ever felt frightened by a headline or angered by a caller on a talk show?

When do you know which stories to believe? What methods do you use to filter lies out of the truth and separate valuable information from spam? How do you guide your own thoughts when there are so many people intent on guiding them for you?

Logic teaches us to check for the "truth" of a fact by evaluating its context, checking the cited authority, noting its frequency and seeking corroboration. Nevertheless, despite obvious image manipulations in videos, movies, TV and commercials, what we see with our own eyes (context) usually convinces most of us that it's real and true, especially if a celebrity (authority) testifies to the worth of a particular brand or an idea. As for frequency and corroboration, thanks to the Internet and every type of social media, within weeks millions of people see and corroborate all sorts of urban legends.

Even if we could effectively evaluate information by these criteria, reliance upon them still leaves us vulnerable to wasting our time and losing our money. Bernard Madoff's Ponzi scheme successfully conned thousands of supposedly savvy investors, smart people who surely relied on at least some if not all of these criteria. Clearly we need a better basis for making decisions, financial and otherwise.

Of course, you probably wouldn't quote as gospel something you heard in a chat room. And, you would probably Google more than one or two sites before putting too much stock in anonymous opinions about a product. But how do you determine what is "true"? How do you know what is really going to be useful for your own life? How do you choose what to believe from all the information, hype and opinions incessantly competing for your attention?

Take three minutes to play the SAYS WHO? Game by answering the following five questions:

1. "Says Who?"*
2. "What emotion does this person want me to feel?"
3. "What action does this person want me to take based on that feeling?"
4. "What does this person gain by my having that feeling and taking that action?"

And the most important question…

5. "Do I want to feel that way and do I want to take that action?"

Can you see now how playing the SAYS WHO? Game, frees you from a plague of worries and unnecessary distractions?

These five questions help you quickly determine whether something is worth the investment of your attention, your money, your time and, especially, your sanity.

Your life time is yours and only yours to invest, waste or give away as you choose. Are you ready to dump the clutter and tune in exclusively to the ideas that serve you best? As you play the SAYS WHO? Game and as you discard what's irrelevant, the authority of your own mind is restored to its rightful place.

Bonus Benefit

*Notice when your answer to "Says Who?" is "They say." Ask yourself, "Am I willing to have my mind and emotions influenced by people I don't know?" If you choose to be influenced by others, be sure to find out who "they" are. Then decide if you really want "them" at the wheel in your mind.

Game #4

Master Hypnotist

It is no exaggeration to say that every human being is hypnotized to some extent, either by ideas he has uncritically accepted from others, or ideas he has repeated to himself or convinced himself are true.

—Maxwell Maltz (1899–1975)
Author/surgeon

You probably agree with the popular notion that our thoughts affect our lives. But, have you actually paid much attention to how what you're thinking is affecting you? If you don't like the way your life is going, I'd guess your answer is no. The MASTER HYPNOTIST Game, a simple exploration of how your thoughts create your experience, is a marvelously easy way to begin enjoying a life much closer to your ideal.

Every professional hypnotist and every advertising executive knows that all they can do is make suggestions. It is the hypnotism subject and the television viewer who, accepting the suggestion, hypnotizes himself. Yet, once captivated by an hypnotic trance, a person will comply with suggestions that are as powerful, and often as ridiculous, as the commands of a stage hypnotist.

So, how does the ad man or the hypnotist (or your mother, teacher, spouse or drill sergeant) persuade you to go along with their suggestions?

That's easy. All they need to do is gain your agreement. And this agreement happens when you repeat their suggestions to yourself using statements that begin with the following phrases:

I think...

I believe...

I know...

and

I am...

When what we say begins with these words, we accept and act on what follows without question, even when those ideas are in direct opposition to our success and happiness. Have you noticed this for yourself?

The great news, however, is that waking from these self-induced trances begins with awareness. So, let's play the MASTER HYPNOTIST Game.

Step 1. The next time you begin a sentence with one of the phrases above, just notice what follows. (Of course, what you'll notice immediately is that you are using these phrases all the time.) This allows you to reevaluate the truth of your statements. You could surprise yourself with opinions and sentiments that haven't been true for you in years. Or, you could find yourself claiming to think, believe or know something that, when you stop to think about it, was never true for you.

Step 2. Use these phrases as triggers to really listen. Ask your ears to "listen up," whenever they hear the words think, believe, know or am come out of your mouth. By simply paying attention to what you claim about yourself, you will much more often make statements that reflect the best that is in you. Imagine just how comfortable you can be with yourself when what you say matches your current experience of who you are.

Bonus Benefit

To understand more accurately what you really do think, believe or know, and to see more clearly who you are, turn each statement into a question:

"Do I think...?"

"Do I believe...?"

"Do I know...?"

And the most magical of all is, "Am I...?"

As you listen attentively to your answers, you could be amazed and excited to discover a brand new story about your very own life.

Game #5

Take Five Trance Awakening

By the power of imagination, all men, certainly imaginative men, are forever casting enchantments, and all men, especially unimaginative men, are continually passing under their power.
—Neville Goddard (1905–1972)
Author/philosopher

Now that you've played the MASTER HYPNOTIST Game, you're ready to learn how to quickly awaken yourself from any unwelcome trance.

Before we look at how to play the TAKE FIVE TRANCE AWAKENING Game, let's talk a bit more about just what an hypnotic trance state actually is. Despite all the hocus-pocus and hype, hypnosis is simply focused attention combined with imagination and either heightened emotion or relaxation.

Test this for yourself. Think about the last time you read a magazine or newspaper. Or, just notice what is happening as you are reading this book. First, the act of looking at words on a page is an example of focused attention. As you look at the page and as you read the text, you are paying much less attention to what else is going on around you.

Next, notice how you use your imagination as you read. Notice how you create an image in your mind based on the words you are reading. For example, when you read the word "tree," your mind immediately uses imagination to formulate a corresponding image.

Then, notice your emotions as you read. Are you feeling curious about what you are learning from this book? Are you feeling a sense of expectation and excitement? Or are you feeling a welcome sense of relaxation just knowing that you won't be helplessly directed by other people's enchantments any more?

Notice, now, as you experience this combination of focused attention, imagination and emotion or relaxation, you are eager to learn more about your own mind. You really want to read on and discover new ways to create and to break hypnotic trances at will.

Whenever focused attention combines with imagination and either heightened emotion or relaxation, you are likely to go into an hypnotic trance state. And, once there, your mind is very susceptible to suggestion and control by other people. Understanding this, could inspire you, even now, to wonder just how often you are in this state on a daily basis.

However, it can also be very useful for your own purposes to be in this state, which is often referred to as "the zone" or "flow." It's much easier to get things done when "in trance" and, surely, you're just fine with being "entranced" often in this way during your day. In fact, it's a great way to tune out what could otherwise distract you from your work or your play. Nevertheless, when you suspect that your mind has been invaded by someone else's enchantment, it could be time to awaken from the trance.

Here are a few of the clues that let you know when that time has come:

1) Your breathing is fast and/or shallow

2) Your attention is fixated on an unpleasant image
3) You're feeling frightened, worried or anxious
4) You desperately imagine you need to fight or flee
5) You are reaching for your drug and not sure why
6) You are slumped in your chair, staring at the TV

So, now, to play the FIVE COUNT TRANCE AWAKENING Game.

Step 1. Take three deep breaths. This will immediately break the intensity of the fight-or-flight impulse. Keep breathing deep, relaxing breaths throughout the game.

Step 2. Turn your attention away from the worrisome object, situation or person. Turn away physically, if possible. If it's not possible to turn your body, then, in your imagination, turn your attention toward something in the opposite direction.

Alternately, keep a small object handy, like a smooth stone or a marble. Then, when you play the FIVE COUNT TRANCE AWAKENING Game, just hold the stone or marble in the palm of your hand, focusing your attention on it.

Step 3. Look at the nearest doorway. Assure yourself that you have the right and the liberty to go out that door whenever you choose. Just knowing that you can get away gives you the freedom of choice to stay and awaken from the trance. (If you happen to be incarcerated, use your imagination to see a doorway, then assure yourself as above. In imagination, you can always go anywhere you choose.)

Step 4. Continue breathing deeply and repeat the following Five Count Trance Awakening exercise.

One – Feeling my body breathing and relaxing.

Two – Feeling my mind clearing and relaxing.

Three – Feeling my wisdom and my strength returning.

Four – Feeling more alert, alive and refreshed.

Five – Feeling completely awake, ready and eager to begin again.

As you feel these feelings and as you return your attention to the situation, notice how much more confident you are. Now that you are relaxed and in control of your emotions, you are again the Master Hypnotist, focusing your attention and using your imagination as you direct them.

Bonus Benefit

Of course, sometimes, the experience of fast and shallow breathing, focused attention and intense emotional sensations (which feel much the same as the fight-or-flight response) is desirable. This is the reason for roller coasters, haunted houses and scary movies, as well as a common consequence of sexual attraction. However, even after those experiences, you may want to play the FIVE COUNT TRANCE AWAKENING Game. This will ensure that you don't go into debt for the Maserati you don't really want to own, even after the salesman let you take it for a test drive.

Game #6

I Get To...

Your life is the sum result of all the choices you make, both consciously and unconsciously. If you can control the process of choosing, you can take control of all aspects of your life. You can find the freedom that comes from being in charge of yourself.
—Robert F. Bennett
U.S. Senator, Utah (1933–)

Do you start your day by thinking about all the things you "have to" do? Do you "have to" get up, "have to" go to work, and then "have to" take care of all the things on your ever-lengthening (have) TO DO list? Have you ever considered how much power you give this simple phrase to trash your happiness?

To live as though you "have to" is to live without free will. Saying that you "have to" incites in the imagination a vision of a marionette forever hanging from strings manipulated by someone else. And, indeed, that can be what it feels like when you are forever doing only what you "have to" do. Then, either in your mind or in your daily affairs, you wage war against those people you imagine are making you do what you "have to" do.

As you learned from playing the MASTER HYPNOTIST Game, you are always your own hypnotist. Whatever you tell yourself becomes the trance you live. Because of this, the language that you use makes your daily life either a drudgery of painful duties or an adventure of self-determined choices. Notice how it feels to think about what you "get to" do. Even when it's exactly the same task, just replacing "have to" with "get to" changes your emotional state and your mental attitude.

Play the I GET TO… Game and see how wondrously simple rewriting your own story can be. Release yourself from the illusion that you "have to" do anything.

Step 1. Whenever you find yourself thinking or saying the words, "I have to…" simply restate the thought, in your head and aloud, "I get to…." Whether it's going to work, going to the bathroom, or even going to war, in all cases, you get to do this thing.

For example, do you really "have to" go to work? The fact is you have a job that you get to go to. Which means, you get to earn a paycheck. You, also, get to use your skills and talents and physical capacities to participate in the world. And, there was a time, however long ago, that you wanted this job, when you got to apply for it and you got to accept it.

Step 2. Whenever you contemplate a new opportunity, say, "I get to…." Awaken within yourself the confidence and courage that accompany conscious choices.

Step 3. Apply the I GET TO… Game to everything you do from taking a drink of water to taking on the world.

Bonus Benefit

To affirm that you are getting to do what you want in the present is great encouragement to believe that you will get to do what you desire in the future.

It's that simple. You get to decide how to live your life.

Game #7

New Thot Box

The true sign of intelligence is not knowledge but imagination.
—Albert Einstein (1879–1955)
Theoretical physicist/philosopher

While playing the SAYS WHO? Game, do you find you're listening more closely to what other people are saying? And after playing the MASTER HYPNOTIST Game, are you more convinced, and a little excited, about the power of your own words to influence yourself?

Playing the NEW THOT BOX Game, you will combine the insights you're gathering from those games and launch your imagination in brand new directions. However, before we play, let's look at exactly what thoughts and words are.

First, consider that every time a person speaks, it is with the intention to influence. This includes the times when there's no one in the room but you. You are always thinking or speaking with the desire to influence those within earshot.

Yet, how often do you hear truly new ideas? How often are people wanting to influence you by repeating decades'-old opinions or yesterday's news? How often do you get a forwarded email claiming that it's hot-off-the-press when it's actually been cycling around the Internet since the turn of the century?

Of course, to consider the seasoned thoughts of others and to share stimulating ideas are joyous and generous activities. Yet, a person spouting ideas that aren't new, at least to himself, is simply a redundant echo of more imaginative people. If you aspire to being a significant and constructive influence in your own and others' lives, it's essential to become aware of and value your own thoughts.

A word about the NEW THOT BOX Game: This is not a game of comparison with the thoughts of others. It does not require high-jumping or a PhD. Set the bar on the floor. As with all the games in this collection, this is a game of non-competitive self-discovery.

Now, reawaken to the unique and creative ideas flowing incessantly through your mind as you play the NEW THOT BOX Game.

Step 1. Get a shoebox, a dozen pens and a pack of 3 × 5 index cards.

Step 2. Separate the cards into a dozen stacks. Put a stack of cards and a pen in/on the following places:

The pocket of your favorite jacket;

Your car's cup holder;

Your bathroom next to the toilet;

Your nightstand;

Your kitchen counter;

Your top desk drawer;

Your TV;

Your gym bag;

Your briefcase;

Your purse;

and anywhere else a new thought can find you.

Step 3. Open your mind and listen. All that is required for an idea to qualify as a "New Thot" is for your mind to link two concepts that it has never linked together before. For example, mohair sneakers, leading a poetry slam in Lithuania, painting your nails with glow-in-the-dark polish.

Step 4. Write whatever your mind imagines on the nearest 3 × 5 index card and place it in the New Thot Box. Then listen some more.

It's possible that you might not have any new thoughts at first. When I began playing the NEW THOT BOX Game, I was stunned to realize how little I was actually "thinking." It seemed that all my thoughts were recycled ideas, song lyrics, news headlines, or someone else's comments just going around and around in my head. If that's true for you, too, just keep listening and keep writing.

In a short time, you will find yourself eager to hear what you alone have to say. Very soon, you will find these new thoughts expanding your choices, enlivening your conversations, leading you to observe and notice your familiar world in a whole new way.

And, most exciting of all, you find that the mind you used to hate, the mind that bored and berated you with its repetitious thinking, freely delivers ideas that enrich your life in undreamed-of ways!

Bonus Benefit

Thinking for yourself and celebrating what you think are grand steps toward expanding your sense of autonomy. All the world's great thinkers dared to listen inwardly first. There, in their own imaginative minds, they discovered the wisdom that guided legions of others into richer, happier, more expanded lives. Awaken to your own imagination and you will influence others to re-friend their own minds. Absolutely nothing is so satisfying to the human mind as formulating its own ideas.

Game #8

Up Until Now...

All things are possible until they are proved impossible—and even then, the impossible may only be so, as of now.
—Pearl S. Buck (1892–1973)
American Pulitzer Prize-winning author

All day, you share your observations of the world, of circumstances, of other people and yourself. And by the conventions of the English language, you probably express these observations in the present tense, i.e., "The day is cloudy," "That car's going fast," "I'm sleepy." However, by the time you've formulated those observations into thoughts or words, the condition you describe is already in the past. Even by the time you are aware of perceiving something through sight, touch, taste, smell or hearing, it has already happened. Every observation you make, therefore, is history.

However, this history is unique to you; it is not universal. It is, also, far from comprehensive. Not only do we perceive the world from our singular point of view, we "perceive" precious little of the information available to us. According to studies in neurological science, our senses receive as many as 70 million bits of stimulus a second. Yet, of that 70 million, the mind consciously processes only 16 to 40 bits. Considering that our observations are based on such a tiny fraction of available information, isn't it a relief to know we can see things differently than we saw them in the past?

When the world interests you, and the people and things in it please you, your descriptions reflect that fascination and pleasure. However, if you hear yourself describing a world you're sick of and a life you want to escape, it's time to move onward with your life.

In just one step, play the UP UNTIL NOW... Game and open the door to a bright new future.

Step 1. When you make any observation that does not glorify, dignify or bring joy to the person, situation or thing, simply begin or end your observation with, "Up until now...." Immediate benefits:

1. "Up until now..." acknowledges that your observation refers to what the situation was and that you recognize it's already in the past;

2. "Up until now..." informs your listener that you are open to new perceptions;

3. "Up until now..." reminds you that things can change.

4. "Up until now..." is useful when you want to discuss your former perceptions or add background information to a situation, while leaving the present open to be different.

5. "Up until now..." acknowledges that your past observations may well have been valid at the time and releases you from the need to defend them.

6. "Up until now..." opens the door to be who you are today, not simply an echo of who you were in the past.

7. Framing your earlier perceptions with "Up until now..." frees you to choose something else more suited to who you are today.

That was then. This is now.

Bonus Benefit

Playing the UP UNTIL NOW… Game, you are probably aware that many of your thoughts about yourself and others originated quite a while ago, maybe even years or decades ago. Some of those thoughts could have been true back then, but they aren't true for you now. You will even discover other thoughts that never were kind, supportive or useful, much less true. The UP UNTIL NOW… Game gives you the perfect opportunity to do some effortless and thorough mind clearing. As you reevaluate your perceptions of yourself and your world, be enchanted by the possibilities opening up in front of you.

Game #9

Use Your Drugs

Happy the man who condemneth not himself in that thing which he alloweth. —King James Bible, Romans 14:22

Got a drug "problem"?
Does just reading that question make you want to light up, eat a bon bon, take a swig? Well, I tell you what... be my guest. I'll wait right here. You go on and satisfy that urge. The USE YOUR DRUGS Game is all about getting the most out of whatever drug, habit, addiction or behavior you've used, up until now, to get this far in life.

And, I mean that in a good way.

Back now? Feeling better? Good.

Now let's play the USE YOUR DRUGS Game. This game is played a bit differently than the previous games. You're invited to consider ideas that might either be new to you or that might confirm what you already know. In any case, there's plenty of time to take breaks and use your drugs while you play along.

We'll start with a review. This could be especially valuable to those who are up that river, you know, the one called De Nile.

> **addict** [L. addictus, pp. of addicere to favor, fr. ad- + dicere to say — more at DICTION] (1534) 1 : to devote or surrender (oneself) to something habitually or obsessively 2 : to cause addiction to a substance.

Now, before we get into actually playing the USE YOUR DRUGS Game, let's even the playing field. Everyone engages in addictive behavior in some way at some time. This, therefore, makes all assertions that "addicts" are a separate population moot. So, don't endure any BS that says you are unique in your depravity or social disgrace. Absolutely no one is exempt, although some of us are just a tad more clever at hiding it.

Considering the infinite variety of substances and behaviors to which people obsessively surrender themselves, would it surprise you to learn that every addiction satisfies its user in exactly the same way? Yes, it's true.

Every addict uses his or her drug for relief from the stressful emotions arising from self-inflicted, erroneous trances about what they believe, think or know or perceive themselves to be.

Here are some examples.

Let's start with the most popularly dissed ones. Excessive sex relieves the sadness of believing you aren't lovable. Excessive stimulants relieve the stress of incessant thinking at the expense of rest and sleep. Excessive smoking relieves the tension of being caught in a place or situation that you imagine you can't escape. Excessive shopping relieves the heart's ache of believing you are not good enough.

And then there are other addictions, some of which you may at first question. Yet each behavior clearly meets the definition of addiction. Excessive TV watching relieves the frustration of not knowing how to influence your world. Excessive reading relieves the despair of believing one's own words aren't important. Excessive formal education relieves the anxiety of doubting one's place in the world.

Who determines what is "excessive"? This determination belongs solely to the individual. No one looking in from the outside can judge this. However, everyone who depends excessively on anything must admit that the substance, activity or distraction more often masks the problem than provides true relief.

Are you one of us? Then, play on!

Step 1. Right now, cut that noose of condemning judgment from around your neck. Use the MASTER HYPNOTIST and UP UNTIL NOW... Games to question those old judgments about yourself and put them squarely behind you. Whatever your past relationships were to particular things or people, recognize and accept that those were your best choices, up until now.

Step 2. Thank yourself for doing what you could to alleviate stress and tension. Those conditions are clearly harmful to your health.

Step 3. Prepare, now, to enjoy your drug of choice by first playing the COME HOME! Game. As you engage with your drug or addictive behavior, do everything you can to really savor the experience. Take it in with the thrill of your very first disorienting puff, orgasmic bite, or intoxicating gulp. Surrender to that activity with complete abandon. Knowing that relief is what you want, give your drug permission to get you as far into balance and the sense of ease and relief as possible.

Step 4. Once your drug has quelled the sensations of stress and tension, ask yourself if you would now prefer to reach a deeper, longer-lasting equilibrium.

If your answer is "No" or "Not yet," then you have played this game as fully as you can for now. Simply repeat Step 3, every time you use your drugs.

If, on the other hand, you are curious about another way to play, move on to Steps 5 and 6.

Step 5. While you are relaxed and calm under the influence of your drug, consider again the word "addiction." It is the union of the prefix ad-, which means "toward or before," and diction, which means "choice of words, especially with regard to correctness, clearness and effectiveness." Thus, the words you chose to speak up until now led you toward your addiction. Now, the key to your deeper, long-lasting equilibrium is your choice of different, more effective, words.

Step 6. Either play all of Step 3. or simply begin by playing the COME HOME! Game. Now, with the clear intention of deepening your sense of balance and equilibrium, invest 10 minutes playing one of the following games:

SAYS WHO?
MASTER HYPNOTIST
TAKE FIVE TRANCE AWAKENING
I GET TO...
MOTHER TONGUE
I'M OUTTA HERE!
PLAY WITH YOURSELF
I AM NOT SORRY!
OFF THE HOOK

Bonus Benefit

Condemnation creates attachment, which is why Step 1 in the USE YOUR DRUGS Game releases you from condemning judgment. Ultimately, detachment and indifference are the states of mind that will be your best allies in releasing yourself from any addiction.

Until then, be consoled by the wisdom of George Fox, founder of the American Society of Friends, or Quakers. In one story about Fox, he is counseling William Penn, founder of Pennsylvania and member of the Society of Friends. Penn was troubled by the inconsistency of wearing a sword as part of his role as a military cavalier with his membership in the nonviolent Society of Friends. With the tolerance and patience that exemplifies Quakerism, Fox said, "When it gets too heavy for thee, thee will put it down."

Game #10

Aim For The Back Of The Head

I don't ever try to hit a man in the face. I always aim for the back of the head. —Muhammad Ali (1942–)
Three-time World Heavyweight Champion

Have you ever had a Big Dream bloom in your mind? The sort of really Big Dream that would take all your resources and most of your time, yet you just knew it was a Great Idea? Then, have you told a friend about it, sure they'd love the idea, too?

But, your "friend" couldn't see into your imagination like you can. Instead, he looked at you with his face pinched up in that expression that says, Are you nuts? Then, after he explained all the reasons why what you wanted to do can't be done, perhaps he tried to console you, advising you not to be so overly ambitious, not to cause yourself heartache by dreaming such Big Dreams.

Did you go on with your Big Dream after that experience? Or did you let that person's attitude puncture your idea like a pin pops a balloon? If you didn't go on with that Big Dream, did you find another even better one, maybe the one that you're living now? Or was that the last dream, big or small, that you've had in a long time... perhaps until now?

If you have started toward an opportunity, a vision, a plan or a Big Dream but have been diverted along the way by the opinions of others, the AIM FOR THE BACK OF THE HEAD Game is for you.

In the boxing ring of life, the back of the head is the achievement and fulfillment of the Big Dream. This is where we want the strength of our ideas and the force of our vision to take us. Big Dreams are never KO'd by the current "realities" of the world. The blow that defeats millions of great ideas is the vapid opinion of a "friend."

But why a friend? Isn't that something only an enemy would do? This death-blow to our dreams comes most often from a friend for two reasons. First, it is to friends we most often confide our dreams. And, second, it is our friends' opinions that we consider most important. However, our friends may lack sufficient faith in their own creativity. And those who don't believe in their own minds are incapable of having faith in anyone else's. The inability to see with imagination blinds a person to seeing anyone else's vision.

The next time you have a Big Dream or a Great Idea, play the AIM FOR THE BACK OF THE HEAD Game, and ensure that your idea blooms into Being!

Step 1. Go to a sporting goods store and buy yourself a pair of boxing gloves. As of this writing, you can get a pair of red or hot pink Everlast gloves at Walmart for under $30. Or, you can order red or black Rocky Costume Gloves for under $20 on Amazon. Have someone help you properly secure the gloves onto your hands. Now, have some fun; dance around and punch the air. Play at being Rocky Balboa or any other boxer you can think of. Feel the protection that the thick padding gives your hands, and the weight that amplifies your swing.

Display your gloves in a prominent place. Although the gloves are meant to be a talisman rather than a tool, be prepared to put them on in the presence of any "friend" who starts to tell you what cannot be done, especially regarding your Big Dream.

Step 2. For the next seven nights, invest the last minute or two before you go to sleep in playing the COME HOME! Game. This time between waking and sleep is called the hypnagogic moment. According to research and mythology, the mind is particularly imaginative during this transitional state. Many great inventors, including Thomas Edison and Henry Ford, intentionally used this time to direct their imaginations.

By ending your day playing the COME HOME! Game, you will help your mind become clear and calm. Then, as you drift into sleep, imagine moving effortlessly into that place and space where your Big Dream is already complete and fulfilled.

Step 3. Also, for the next seven days, keep a stack of index cards and a pen handy. With your mind devoted to imagining the fulfillment of your Big Dream, play the NEW THOT BOX Game. Write at least one new thought each day that develops and enhances your vision of the fulfillment of your Great Idea. Don't be too surprised to find yourself writing more, possibly a lot more, than one card a day.

Step 4. At the end of the week, accumulate your cards, go to a private place, get comfortable, and begin again with a minute or two of the COME HOME! Game. Now, read over your cards. Do you notice how the additional thoughts you wrote during the week have developed the vision of the fulfillment of your Big Dream even more? Notice as you read the cards and as you think about your Big Dream, achieved and fulfilled, how its colors, its sounds and smells, textures and light, and, especially, its reality come into sharper focus.

Step 5. Imagine yourself standing squarely in the middle of your Big Dream after it has been achieved and fulfilled. Again, pay close attention to the sensory details, the colors, the sounds, the smells, textures and light. Notice, too, how your body feels standing in the middle of the fulfilled Big Dream. Do you feel warm or cool, at ease or excited? On an index card, write a description of this experience from this perspective of standing in the middle of that scene. Use rich details so that you will be there in your mind every time you read the card.

Step 6. Keep this card with you and read it at least once daily. Carry it with you over the next days, weeks or months while your Big Dream unfolds. And unfold in your world, it must, now that it is real in your mind. As the Big Dream manifests, the right people, also, show up to help it come to life.

However, keep those boxing gloves handy and obvious. Let everyone else, including your "friends," know that they are in easy reach. You may not be planning to knock anyone out. But, as you master the art of aiming for your wish fulfilled, those gloves will remind those with opinions to the contrary that they'd better just shut the @#&* up.

Bonus Benefit

Get some real use out of the boxing gloves. Check out the Internet for free online boxing pointers or check out a library book on boxing. Better yet, find a local boxing gym. Spar with a punching bag. Practice some fancy footwork. Learn how to feint and jab. Consider replacing some or all of your existing gym workout with cardio-boxing. [Just seeing you do this can be enough to shut up most of your critics.]

Then, if you have a moment when the speed of your approaching Big Dream feels too slow or you're feeling less than powerful, strap on those hot pink gloves. Go a round or two with your shadow while your mind calms down. "Float like a butterfly, sting like a bee," as Ali would say.

Section Two

Going Deeper

Now that you've given yourself a respite from anxiety, now that you've enjoyed moments of welcome relief, you may be rousing from the trance that life is a punishment to be endured.

If this is the case, play on. In the next ten games, we look more closely at the games you're already playing that trash your happiness. And, with each you are given the antidote — new games to play to waken even more fully into the life you were meant to live with the mind you were given to use.

Game #11

Mother Tongue
Speaking the Language of Heaven, Hell or Purgatory

In the beginning was the Word, and the Word was with God, and the Word was God. —King James Bible, John 1:1

Dear Reader, I hope that playing these games is encouraging you to appreciate your own thoughts. I also hope you've come to see that the mind you wanted to "shut the @#&* up" really has some pretty good ideas. It wouldn't surprise me, either, if you've begun to notice how much of this reconnection with your own mind is all about words. And, I dearly hope you are truly excited about this.

Before we jump right into playing the MOTHER TONGUE Game, let's look a bit more at just how words, specifically adjectives, create our worlds. Mark Twain said, "A man's character may be learned from the adjectives which he habitually uses in conversation." Now, don't sweat it, this isn't a test. If you've been faking it all these years, pretending to know an adjective from an adverb or a participle or any other part of speech, your secret's safe with me. Here's a definition, so we can pretend you knew it all along. And, after you play the MOTHER TONGUE Game, you're going to be a master in the use of adjectives.

> **adjective** : a word serving as a modifier of a noun to denote a quality of the thing named, to indicate its quantity or extent, or to specify a thing as distinct from something else.

Before we get further into a discussion of adjectives, I'd like to share with you why this game is named MOTHER TONGUE. It's because the language we use literally gives birth to the worlds we live in. And this perception of the world directly determines how we live our lives within it.

"In the beginning was the word." Now, the issue here isn't that this quote is from a book you may or may not like. The issue is that the word, your word, is the beginning of everything you experience. And those words that go forth out of your mouth do not return to you empty-handed. The evidence of your words surrounds you every day. And that means, it's entirely up to you whether the world encircles you in a community of friends, encases you in a stupefying fog or closes in on you like a pack of wolves.

So, in what world would you say your sweet life is taking place right now? Are you happy in Heaven? Are you treading water in Purgatory? Or are you, like Prometheus, having your guts ripped out every day in Hell?

If you know the answer and you want to change your residence, or you know the answer but you don't know why, it's time to play MOTHER TONGUE: Speaking the Language of Heaven, Hell or Purgatory Game.

Step 1. Take a piece of lined notebook paper and fold it into thirds lengthwise. Along the top of the page, write HEAVEN in the left column, HELL in the center and PURGATORY in the right.

Step 2. Keep the paper with you. Whenever you notice yourself using an adjective, write it in the appropriate column.

(If you don't have a certain sense of the difference between these states, here's my way of determining. Heaven is where everything is possible and getting better, Hell is where whatever awfulness is happening is only going to get worse and Purgatory is where no change is possible.)

Step 3. For every word you enter in its appropriate column, write another adjective in each of the other two columns, words that you could use to modify the same noun. For example, if you write, "bland" as a description of a meal in the PURGATORY column, you might write, "delicious" in the HEAVEN column and "disgusting" in the HELL column. "But," you insist, "it's true, the food is bland!" It's okay for now if you want to stick with your words. At this point, you're just noticing what other words you could use to describe your experience. I'm confident, too, that at some point in this game, you begin to get the idea about how simply changing an adjective can change your world.

Here's an example of my own lists:

HEAVEN	HELL	PURGATORY
lovely	ugly	flawed
eager	frantic	apathetic
friendly	friendless	online dating
kind	cruel	rude
happy	angry	numb
comfortable	pissed off	awkward
helpful	helpless	hopeless
accepting	disgusted	dissatisfied

Step 4. Once you've filled up the whole page, cut or rip the page along the fold between HEAVEN and HELL, and throw away the HELL and PURGATORY columns. Relax. You

know these words by heart, so you can always use them in the future. Just keep in mind where they'll take you when you do.

Step 5. Make multiple copies of your HEAVEN list, then keep a copy in every location listed for your NEW THOT BOX Game index cards. Be sure to keep copies by your phone and computer.

Step 6. Integrate your HEAVEN words into your writing, your phone calls, your emails, your speeches, your reports, your conversations, and especially, ESPECIALLY, your thoughts. Then, stand back and watch the transformation of your world right before your eyes.

Bonus Benefit

Here's an old joke that's an example of the difference between Heaven and Hell based on generalities about cultures. If you laugh in agreement, it means that you've been conditioned to believe in those characterizations, just like the rest of us. However, now that you are re-creating your own Heaven, you can laugh along with the joke without falling into the trance.

Heaven is when you have:
An American salary
A British home
Chinese food
A Swiss economy
An Italian body
Japanese technology
An African tool
An Indian wife

Hell is when you have:
An American wife
A British body
A Chinese tool
Swiss food
Italian technology
A Japanese home
An African economy
An Indian salary

Game #12

I'm Outta Here!
Cancelling Your Membership In The Scared S**tless Club

Inaction breeds doubt and fear. Action breeds confidence and courage. If you want to conquer fear, do not sit home and think about it. Go out and get busy.

—Dale Carnegie (1888–1955)
American lecturer/author

Imagine yourself sitting comfortably in a quiet place somewhere. Maybe you're in your own house in your favorite chair, or outside in the warm sun. Imagine a good friend is nearby, and there's soft music playing. You're feeling pretty peaceful, relaxed, in a good space.

Then, you hear a voice. It could be a voice on the radio or the TV. It could be your friend's voice. It could even be one of the many voices inside your own head. And this voice says something scary, something like one of these headlines:

NYC terrorism suspect cites subway attack plan
Gasoline heading above $5 a gallon by this summer
Toyota misled public on safety problem
Jobless rates increase in 29 states
Four women among dead in suicide bombing at market

That's all it takes. Before you can even think of playing the SAYS WHO? Game, that sweet moment of relaxation, that bit of peace is GONE! In a heartbeat, you have been blasted from Heaven to Hell, right down into the crowded lobby of the Scared S**tless Club.

But wait! What's even more amazing is, you want to hear more! You turn your head to listen, or you turn up the volume. What's up with that? Just the first few words cost you your peace, and, now, you're asking for more? Let's look at why.

The primary purpose of a scary news broadcast or headline is to make you, the listener or reader, feel strong emotion, and the easiest emotion to trigger is fear. What can incite you to feel fear about something that happened across town or across the country? Your fear gets triggered when an idea causes you to believe that your basic needs are not getting met. However, the most successful broadcasts and headlines cause you to imagine that what you have right now, you're going to lose. And, the more imminent they can make that loss, the stronger your fear.

To be told that you can't have what you currently don't have can be bad news. Nevertheless, at least, you're surviving as you are. So, the trick is to persuade you to believe that the awful thing that happened somewhere else to someone else is going to happen to you or, in some way, cause you to lose what you have. When you are convinced of that, fear detonates, wiping out any other state of mind you were just enjoying.

Of course, when the dire news we hear is really true and does have a direct impact on our lives, then, responding immediately can make the difference between life and death. The survival urge is powerful for just this reason.

But, when reported events don't relate directly or immediately to your survival, being incessantly triggered to respond fearfully robs you of one of your most essential basic needs: security. Fear is the antithesis of security. Therefore, long before you hear the full story, the alarming headline has robbed you of your peace. You plummet into the Scared S**tless Club, where you join legions of other people running around desperately seeking their lost security.

It's here, in the Club, in that moment of desperation and fear, when you are most vulnerable to hypnotic suggestions. This is the moment when suggestions about how to spend your money, your thoughts and your time can most successfully grab hold of your defenseless mind. But, we'll get to them in a minute, right before we play the I'M OUTTA HERE! Game.

First, let's explore the concept of needs. Although there are a number of ideas about how human needs are organized, I'm going to use the model created by American psychologist Abraham Maslow. In 1943, Maslow presented a paper entitled, *Theory of Human Motivation,* which included his Hierarchy of Needs.

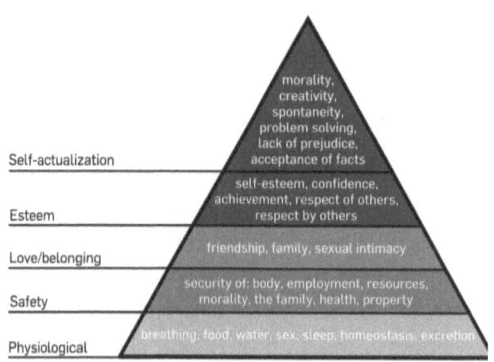

http://en.wikipedia.org/wiki/Maslow's_hierarchy_of_needs

Maslow's premise was that people will do what they must to meet the lower levels of needs before they invest their resources in the higher levels. Thus, at the lowest Physiological level, keeping the body alive and functioning is the most basic need. The second level is Safety, the security of body, employment, resources, morality, the family, health and property.

Now, stop right here. Look again at these headlines:
NYC terrorism suspect cites subway attack plan
Gasoline heading above $5 a gallon by this summer
Toyota misled public on safety problem
Jobless rates increase in 29 states
Four women among dead in suicide bombing at market

Do you notice how many aspects of the lower two levels of needs are threatened? Can you see that there's a threat to every aspect of the Safety level embedded in each headline? Is it any wonder then, that you felt like you simply had to hear more? And, do you realize that as long as your attention is kept on these lower levels, you can forget about even trying to meet your higher needs?

So, what are you missing out on?

The third level is Love and Belonging. Here's where you connect with others as a close family, through friendships and in romantic attachments. The desire to be part of social, religious and community groups is fulfilled here.

The fourth level is Esteem. At this level, a person feels respected and recognized by others, while also enjoying self-respect, competence and confidence. Here's where you gain the most from playing the SAYS WHO?, I GET TO… and UP UNTIL NOW… Games.

The fifth level is Self-Actualization. Here's where the Big Dream lives. At this level, you develop the thoughts you've discovered with the NEW THOT BOX Game. Here's where you feel a sense of self-worth and eagerly offer your ideas to the world.

So, are you inclined to come to the defense of the news? After all, just like the *New York Times* masthead claims, All the news that's fit to print. You're probably thinking, so how does scaring me s**tless serve the news media?

To answer that, let's first consider who pays for the news. It's not you. It's advertisers. Now, let's go back to that moment when you plummeted into the Scared S**tless Club. Remember the definition of hypnosis from the FIVE COUNT TRANCE AWAKENING Game? Hypnosis is focused attention combined with imagination and either heightened emotion or relaxation. The hypnosis happened when the words you heard caught your attention, you imagined your own safety was threatened and you felt the fear.

It works just like a one-two punch. The fear trance is cast by the news and, while your mind is running from the fabricated threat, the advertisement or the commercial appears and promises a product that will return you to the security you desperately seek.

Are you getting the idea that a whole lot of the voices you've been wanting to shut the @#&* up don't even belong to you? Are you gratified to see that you really can live above their influence? Does it make sense to you now to revoke your membership in the Scared S**tless Club?

Play the I'M OUTTA HERE! Game, and restore your security to its rightful place — in your control.

Step 1. Set your own intentions. In other words, gain a clear understanding of what you have in mind to do and be. As you slip off to dreamland in your hypnagogic moment, ask yourself "What are my intentions?" Then, when you wake up in the morning, write your answers on an index card.

Intentions are different from goals. You are not looking for hard-won, specific achievements here. What you are exploring are the thoughtful and deliberate directions you wish to travel in your life. You are discovering your deeper purposes. Examples of possible intentions are the concepts listed in the upper three levels of Maslow's Hierarchy of Needs.

Step 2. Keep that intention in your mind as you go out into your day. The easiest way to keep it in your mind is to keep the index card in your pocket. Staying mindful of your own intentions is a powerful deterrent to the distraction of headlines, gossip and other bad-news trances.

Step 3. Turn off the news. Okay, okay. Not forever, though that's not really such a bad idea. But, for now, select a particular time of day to turn off the distractions. Then, every day, for the next week, disconnect yourself from all the tendrils of media that have attached themselves to your brain. Your computer, your radio, TV, TiVo, iPhone, cell phone, all of it.

Step 4. Take 21 minutes and go out for a walk with your own mind. Talk over the ways you would like to develop and experience your intentions. Listen attentively. Take notes. Say "Thank you."

Step 5. On the seventh day, select one of those ways. Decide on one action you can take in 21 minutes or less that will move you along this chosen way, then, take that action. For example, if your intention is to develop self-esteem, complete a step in a project that you and others are relying upon. If your intention is to develop love and belonging, send a postcard of appreciation to a family member.

Now, I don't expect that, right now, you get so excited by this game you turn off all your electronic communication devices forever. I know that doesn't serve your other needs or even make sense. The idea isn't to cut yourself off from the world; the idea is to live with consciously chosen intention in the world. As you develop your intentions, and as you take time with your mind, not only will you be more able to assess what news relates to your safety and what doesn't, you also bring to your life and the lives of others news of exciting possibilities.

Bonus Benefit

Once you begin to choose your own intentions for how you really want to invest your attention, your time and your life, it's easier to free yourself from the trances cast by others. Also, when you accept that it's just their job, there's no need to waste time criticizing journalists and advertising copywriters for making a fine living doing everything they can to snag your attention.

But, make no mistake, those who write that scary news and irresistible ad copy don't just hope to motivate people to feel what they want them to feel and buy what they want them to buy. They positively know they can and will do this. So, as you repeatedly play Step 3, let your media-free time expand. Free your mind to meet your higher needs and serve your own chosen intentions.

Game #13

About-Face!
Moving *Toward* What You Really Want

I have known a great many troubles, but most of them never happened.
—Mark Twain (1835–1910)
American author/humorist

Have you ever made an important decision because you wanted to avoid trouble? Have you ever imagined that going after something you wanted also meant you had to do something that scared you, so you didn't do it? Have you ever let a news report about the weather or traffic convince you not to do something you'd wanted to do?

Do you think that if you just had the courage of Indiana Jones or an Iron Man suit or a real-life Lightsaber you could actually achieve your Big Dream? Do you believe you'd really go for what your heart desires, if the world weren't such a difficult, scary or downright dangerous place?

If you've played a round or two of the I'M OUTTA HERE Game, you might be questioning whether the world really is all that scary or dangerous. And yet, without being aware of it, you could be nurturing that belief by your habitual misuse of language.

If you grew up on this planet, the avoidance response was established in your mind even before you spoke your first words. It is commonly believed among those who study human behavior that babies are born fearing only two things: falling and loud noises. However, in their attempt to direct and control the behavior of children, adults nurture fear of just about everything else. Using negative suggestion, a parent, teacher or any other authority can make a child obey, at least for awhile. For example, two very effective negative suggestions are "Don't!" and "Stop!"

Imagine a 5-year-old playing in the front yard. His mother calls out, "Don't run into the street!" However, since she knows that the child doesn't understand the physics of kid versus car, she warns, "If you do, I'll spank you."

Now, the little boy knows what being spanked is and he knows he doesn't want that. So, the mother cleverly links running into the street with a punishment she knows the boy wants to avoid, and Shazaam! he stays out of the street.

Linking actions to painful consequences — in effect, invoking fear — is an effective way to control a child. For the parent or teacher with a limited toolset, this is often the favorite method of control. As Abraham Maslow said, "If the only tool you have is a hammer, you tend to see every problem as a nail." Therefore, even when a particular action is not harmful in itself, the adult who would be annoyed or inconvenienced by it simply links that action to a painful consequence the child wants to avoid.

Negative suggestions from childhood often stay with a person for life. Being conditioned to respond instantaneously to "Don't!" and "Stop!" can certainly save us from real danger. However, when the majority of our actions are indiscriminately linked to painful consequences, the result is a perception of the world as a very dangerous place.

Playing the ABOUT-FACE! Game redirects your attention toward opportunities and possibilities within a world of relative safety. As with many of the games in this book, simply paying attention to what you say, and then making a small change in your words can turn your life in a brand-new direction, from exactly where you stand today.

Step 1. At the top of five NEW THOT BOX index cards write "ACTION:_____." Below that, write "Because." Keep these cards with you for the next few days.

Step 2. Whenever you take an action, any sort of action, write what it is at the top of the card. For example, "going to the gym," "taking an aspirin," "cleaning out my closet." Then ask yourself, "Why am I doing this?"

Step 3. Following "Because" write your answer on the card. Using the examples above, your answers might be, "Because I don't want to get flabby," "Because I want to get rid of this headache," or "Because I hate this mess."

Step 4. After you've filled out five cards, sit down somewhere by yourself and read them over. Notice how many of your reasons for taking action were to avoid something. Looking at the examples above, "don't want to" indicates avoidance of an unpleasant future consequence, while "want to get rid of," and "hate" indicate the desire to end or avoid current unpleasant circumstances.

If your answers include "I have to," you may want to play another round of the I GET TO… Game,. Feeling that you "have to" do something comes from a belief that you are driven by external forces. Embedded in "have to" is the child-instilled fear of needing to comply. Thus, to avoid punishment, we do what we "have to."

Step 5. On the back of each card, write a reason that moves you *toward* a future consequence you *do* want. Look for reasons that are just as true, or even truer, than those you originally used. Playing with the examples above, you might go to the gym because it feels good to move your body and you like to keep it toned. You could take the aspirin because you want to feel better as fast as possible. You clean your closet to make room for a new wardrobe and to donate your clothes to others.

Step 6. Continue listening to what you say following "because" and its alternates, "so," "in order to" and "for that reason."

Every day, the way you use these statements determines whether the world you live in expands or contracts. Recognizing the benefits inherent in your current choices helps you reestablish a more balanced perception of the world, where expanding experiences and enjoying the process are restored as natural and normal occurrences.

Bonus Benefit

Draw a circle the size of a quarter in the center of a piece of paper. Inside the circle is everything familiar to you, your comfort zone. Outside the circle is the world you haven't explored or experienced yet. Outside the circle write five experiences, adventures or new skills that you want to add to your life.

On another piece of paper, write the numbers 1-20 down the left side. Now, write sensations that you have experienced when you began something new and unfamiliar. List them by increasing intensity. For example, #1 could be "butterflies in my stomach," #2 "sweaty palms," #3 "fidgety," and on up to #20. Make #20 the worst thing that ever happened to you when you tried something new. This is your *Carpe Diem List*.

Choose one of the five experiences you wrote as being outside of your comfort zone. Now, pretend you're taking the next step toward incorporating this experience in your life. Vividly imagine yourself, right now, doing whatever that next action is. Notice how you feel when you imagine taking this action. Since you are going outside your comfort zone, it makes perfect sense to feel a little *un*comfortable. Decide which number from your *Carpe Diem List* matches what you feel. Note that number next to the experience.

As you imagine taking action toward your desire and as you realize that the sensations you might feel are actually familiar and manageable, can you sense your comfort zone expanding? Repeat the game with each of your other experiences. As you see just how doable the next step for each experience is, your decision now is simply to choose which step you take first.

As the author Ayn Rand wrote in *The Fountainhead*, "Throughout the centuries there were men who took first steps, down new roads, armed with nothing but their own vision." Take these steps now and join those fortunate ones whose lives are guided by their own vision.

Game #14

Re-spect
"What Else Do I See?"

Boredom is the result of insufficient attention to detail.
—Unknown

Condemnation, like boredom, is also the result of insufficient attention to detail. How much information do you collect before you condemn, malign or dismiss someone else? Do you ever stop to ask yourself if you really know enough to judge another person? In this era of sound bites, tweets, email blasts, and text messages, how often is your decision to respect or diss someone based on 120 words or less?

Yet, have you ever noticed that when you condemn someone, you've got to defend your judgment? And, did you realize that the harsher your condemnation, the more energy you have to spend to defend it? The really exhausting part, however, is that once you've formed a condemning judgment about someone, it can be frustratingly difficult to fight your way out of your own opinion.

After playing at least a few of these games, are you beginning to get the idea that life is just too short to keep squandering it on this type of sport? As you are enjoying, more and more, the company of your own mind, and, as you are developing your own creative ideas, the issue isn't who can you keep imprisoned in the dungeon of condemning judgment. Your opportunity now is to play your own way out of the dungeon and leave the door open for everyone else to follow you out.

Consider how much genuine interest and compassion you can experience by paying just a little more attention to the people in your life. Imagine how much more comfortable you can be in anyone's company when you're ready to see them for who they are. There's no limit to the benefits you can reap when you give a few extra minutes to seeing the valuable qualities and attributes of those around you.

The great news is that, to start enjoying these benefits, all it takes is respect. Of course, you're familiar with the definition:

> **respect** : (n) high or special regard: ESTEEM;
> (vt) to consider worthy of high regard

But, are you aware of the etymology of the word? Respect derives from the Latin word *respectus,* the act of looking back, and *respicere,* to look back, regard. Therefore, in this game, you have the opportunity to re-spect — to look at again and to re-gard — those people you were first inclined to condemn, diss or ridicule. In this act of looking back, or simply continuing to look, you can open the door to sincere respect. Playing the RE-SPECT Game also gives you an easy way to look back and re-value anyone you condemned in the past.

Step 1. Right now, look up from this book. Glance around until you see something "wrong" with a person in your view. Do you see someone with an awful haircut? Does the guy on the treadmill sing out loud along with his iPod? Is the checkout clerk wasting time chatting with a customer?

Step 2. Take another look and ask yourself, "What else do I see?" Notice five additional physical features about this person or object. These could be colors, textures, sizes or shapes. For example, he has brown shoes, wears glasses, has a goatee, a green tie, a white shirt. As you notice each feature, touch the fingertips of one hand as a way of keeping track.

Step 3. Now notice five details about each of those five observations. For example, his shoes are leather with double-stitching, black soles, one frayed shoelace, and scuff marks on the toe of the right shoe. Again, keep count on your fingertips. Are you getting the idea how long it can take to get a really good look at someone? And, would these 25 observations really be sufficient to make an accurate or reliable judgment about the person?

Step 4. Now, look further. This time, as you ask yourself "What else do I see?" look with the intention of seeing five qualities, features or aspects about the person that you could respect or value. Again, keep track of your observations on your fingertips.

Step 5. Reflect on how playing this game has modified your initial assessment. Has that quality you saw as "wrong" lost its significance? Do you notice how feeling respect for others frees you to allow them to be in the world, without your condemnation? Remember, the purpose here is to release you from the claws of condemning judgment, to free your mind to serve your dreams.

The RE-SPECT Game is also useful to free us from old condemnations that are holding our minds hostage. Here's how to play the game within your imagination.

Step 6. Sit in a quiet place with an index card and a pen. Take one minute to play the COME HOME! Game. Then bring to mind someone you judged in the past whom you still consider "wrong."

Step 7. Picture that person standing in front of you. Ask yourself, "What else do I see?" On one side of the card, write five attributes or qualities you know about the person, in addition to the quality you had judged. Look again. Re-spect. Wouldn't it be curious to discover that you don't know five other true facts or specific details about that person?

Step 8. On the back of the card, write five qualities that you could respect or value in the person. Keep looking. What you may find is, the less you really know about this person, the more the qualities you list are those you have in common, i.e., a human being doing the best he can; a mother/father/sister/son; a person hoping to achieve her goal. Simply recognizing that you are more alike than you are different can be enough to lessen and even erase the desire to condemn.

Bonus Benefit

Despite what you may have been taught and unquestioningly believed for years, life is *not* a competition sport. Life is an opportunity for each and every human being to experience her or his self-written story in multi-dimensional form.

As you look out into the world, imagine you are a judge at the Olympics. As soon as you're tempted to judge someone, reach for your Olympic numbers.

Alas! what's this? Only one card? Yep! and it's a -10-. Now play the RE-SPECT Game. Keep looking at or thinking about the person you're judging until you see one quality that you respect at a level of 10, or even better.

-10- the only Olympic number you'll ever need.

Game #15

Play With Yourself
Producing, Writing and Directing… as well as Starring in Your Life

But men must know, that in this theatre of man's life it is reserved only for God and angels to be lookers on.
—Sir Francis Bacon (1561–1626)
English philosopher/statesman/scientist

Have you ever wanted to stop being You? Have you ever changed your hairstyle, your weight, your job or your spouse, in the hopes that this would change You? Have you ever just flat-out cut and run, hoping to outrun You?

Did anyone ever teach you how to play with yourself? Did anyone ever brag to you about how his own happy life is the result of playing with himself? In those secret moments, when you were somehow supposed to figure this all out on your own, did you ever turn on the lights to see exactly how you played with yourself?

The PLAY WITH YOURSELF Game gives you a way to get more delight out of being You, plus an opportunity to *do it* in front of an audience.

Step 1. THE PRODUCER – Decide on an event in the near future where you want to shine. In your imagination, look at the various scenes in the event — beginning, middle, end. Then choose one scene. It could be as you are welcomed in the door, in the midst of the day's exciting activity, or right after the completion of a successful outcome.

Step 2. THE WRITER – Imagine one line of dialogue you will say in that scene that proves the scene goes just the way you want it. The easier to memorize, the better. Later on, you can incorporate a Shakespearean monologue, if you like. However, for your first few times playing the PLAY WITH YOURSELF Game, imagine something short. "Thank you," is great and can work in almost any scene. So can, "Isn't this grand!" or "What fun to be here!"

Step 3. THE DIRECTOR – Now envision the details of the scene: the set, the lighting, the costumes, the props, the supporting cast. Then, decide on the blocking, meaning, Which door do you walk through? Where are the other characters? What is the sequence of the action?

Step 4. THE STAR – Once you've completed the work of the Producer, the Writer and the Director, it's time to rehearse the Star's part. Memorize the short script. Then walk through the scene in your imagination until you could do it in your sleep. In fact, that's a great idea: do it in your sleep, too. Utilize that marvelous, just-before-sleep, hypnagogic moment.

NOTE ABOUT THE STAR: The better rehearsed your Star, the more certain you are that the scene will be successful. When you know your lines by heart, if a supporting actor flubs his lines, or a prop is missing, or something doesn't go quite like it did in rehearsal, your Star can ad-lib, and carry the scene to its intended and happy conclusion.

Step 5. THE HOUSE MANAGER – This individual has an integral part in the success of your play. By directing the ushers, the ticket takers and the doormen, the House Manager ensures that no disruptive rowdies stay in the theatre.

NOTE ABOUT YOUR AUDIENCE: Long before the houselights go down and your play begins, decide who will sit in the front row. Make sure that you see only smiling and enthusiastic faces beyond the footlights. If you've forgotten to attend to this in advance, ask the House Manager to remove anyone in the theater who doesn't want the best for you. (Since this is *your* House Manager, he or she will know exactly who these malcontent detractors are.)

Once those distracting people are gone, peek through the curtain. Notice, with a thrill, that the theater is filled to capacity. Notice the looks of eager anticipation on everyone's face. Then, notice their wings. Yep, it's your angel audience! Here's the news: they've had their eye on you since the day you were born. They've been watching you and cheering you on since the beginning. They have always known that you have always done the best you could do and, for them, whatever you do is an Oscar-worthy performance. Now, whatever your religious beliefs or non-beliefs are, up until now, just play with this vision and experience what it feels like.

Step 6. It's show time! Dress up your Star to the nines and go to the real event, excited to play this scene. As the curtain rises, wink at the Producer, Playwright, Director and House Manager standing in the wings and smiling at you. Then, go ahead — PLAY WITH YOURSELF, in front of God and everybody.

Bonus Benefit

In the middle of your former performances, did you ever ask yourself, "How much longer is this going to last?" Did you ever feel as though the battle scenes just went on and on and on? Have you waited (along with Godot) for something — anything -- to change? If you've ever lived in Purgatory, you know what it's like when everything just drags on forever.

First, ask yourself, "How long is this drama?" Even if you're right in the middle of a real-life scene, this question reminds you that you are the Producer and the Director of your life.

Next, step out of this scene as soon as you can, and play the COME HOME! Game. Relax your sweet mind.

Then, for the next week, on your NEW THOT BOX index cards, write your answers to the question, "How long is this drama?" It will come clear to you, that, when you're ready, your drama must end. Now, get ready, choose a day, set the scene with your PRODUCER, WRITER, DIRECTOR and ACTOR, play out the last scene in your mind, then end each of your dramas as fast as you can.

If any answer tells you that your culture, your gender, your age or some other external factor requires you to remain caught in some un-fun scene, play the SAYS WHO? Game. If your answers insist that you have to play out your life a certain way, play the I GET TO... Game and see what other options come up. And, if your answers demand that you stay in that drama for the rest of your life, leap ahead to the PAID IN FULL! Game.

I wonder if you are already feeling a renewed thrill and excitement in being You. Maybe you'd even like to jump ahead to the SKATING AWAY FROM THE WALL Game to explore more about authoring the other details of your own magnificent life. And, I would venture to guess, you are realizing another great value in this Bonus Benefit exercise. When a person understands how to shorten time, then she also knows how to lengthen time. So, now you can, at will, enjoy the full extent of pleasure that comes when you PLAY WITH YOURSELF.

Game #16

If I Lived in a Vacuum...
Disengaging from the Joneses

Negotiate with yourself first.
—Dr. Chester L. Karrass
Founder, *Effective Negotiation* Seminars

Once upon a time, I spent a month traveling around New Zealand by bus with my then husband Gordon. Every town we passed through had its "must see" attractions (or, in some of the dinkier towns, its "must see" attraction).

The owners of these attractions had, apparently, cut deals with the regional bus drivers. As we would approach a little burg, the driver waxed poetic over the PA system about the upcoming attraction. Each one was described as even more spectacular than the last sheep station or specialty tea-and-collectibles shop that we'd seen an hour earlier.

As we were heading south one afternoon, our driver announced, "Get ready now to see Te Anau, 'Caves of Rushing Wahtah'." While we approached the town, the driver continued to entice us with visions of a mysterious underground grotto, drifting in silent darkness, surrounded by millions of luminous, shimmering glowworms. And throughout the description, he would intone the mantra, "Caves of Rushing Wahtah." It was powerful. When the bus stopped, all forty bus riders disembarked, chanting "Caves of Rushing Wahtah" as we headed in the direction of this irresistible attraction.

However, I had to go to the loo. While I was there, I decided to play my newly invented game, IF I LIVED IN A VACUUM.... Amazingly, just one round of the game was enough to snap me out of the driver's trance. Coming out of the loo into the afternoon sun, I strode off in the opposite direction from the tour group and went on my own quest to glimpse the elusive Cyanoramphus auriceps, or Kakariki, the yellow-crowned parakeet. And, thus, I escaped with my time and the ten dollar entrance fee to the Caves. This was the first of hundreds of hours and thousands of dollars I have saved by playing the IF I LIVED IN A VACUUM...Game.

Have you ever found yourself on vacation, standing in a crowd around some "must-see" wonder just because a travel brochure said it was the thing to do? Have you ever found yourself surrounded by tourists vying for a glimpse of the Mona Lisa, a ride on the London Eye, or your turn to be photographed beside the Princess Di statue at Madame Tussauds Waxworks, only to remember that you really don't like art, you're terrified of heights and the smell of all those wax bodies is making you ill?

Are you ready to do more of what you want to do, and less of what you think others will envy you for doing? Would you like to invest your future hours and dollars pursuing the interests that fascinate only you? Are you excited by the idea of coming home from your vacation with stories no one but you can tell, about discoveries you alone have made?

Welcome to the IF I LIVED IN A VACUUM... Game where you can quickly determine what choice you really want to make next, whether you're away on vacation or here at home.

Step 1. At the first suggestion of an upcoming adventure, ask yourself, *"If I lived in a vacuum, would I make this choice?"* In other words, *"Would I invest my time and money on this, if no one else ever knew about it?"* If your answer to both these questions is a resounding "Yes!" then go and have a blast!

Step 2. If you're hesitant about your answer to Step 1. ask yourself, *"Who do I intend to brag to about this, and will that person, then, really like me more?"* If you come up with a name and you really believe the person will, indeed, like you more, you might want to play a round of the AIM FOR THE BACK OF THE HEAD Game. Whenever someone else's opinion makes you hesitate to invest in the life you really want to live, that's an indication your focus has drifted from your Big Dream. You could also revisit Step 1 of the I'M OUTTA HERE! Game to remind yourself of your intentions.

Step 3. Ask yourself what you'd rather do. If at least one idea doesn't leap to mind, or if you draw a blank, it's time to renew your daily play in the NEW THOT BOX Game. There is no better time than now to discover, or rediscover your own choices.

As you invest your time only in experiences that truly interest you, your increasing self-confidence will earn you more respect than going along with the crowd ever could. Someone else's envy, disinterest or dismissal can't affect the deep satisfaction of doing what you love. So, before you spend another hundred bucks or one more day of your life doing *anything*, ask yourself, *"If I lived in a vacuum, would I make this choice?"* Listen for the answer from your own heart and mind. What are you truly eager to experience? What are you curious about at this moment? What are you longing to explore or invest in right now?

Bonus Benefit

Now, I understand there are those among you who are already committed to saving your money and following your own path. However, you still want to brag about seeing the Pieta in St. Peter's Basilica, bungee-jumping in Queenstown, or joining the Mile-High Club on a flight back from Hawaii, even when you didn't.

Well, this is where your developing creative imagination can really kick in, especially when you're telling stories about traveling to distant places. Oh, and, by the way, you'll be in very good company. Wikipedia describes Il Milione, Marco Polo's account of his travels over the Silk Road in the 13th century, as "translated, embellished, copied by hand and adapted; there is no authoritative version." So, who knows how much of what Marco Polo claimed to have actually seen and done he just heard about around a campfire somewhere?

Today, if you want to create a story of your travels (real or creative), resources for checking out a place or an event are unlimited. YouTube, MySpace, FaceBook, and StreetView, for starters. With the Internet, it's possible to learn more details about a well-known place than most casual visitors ever see.

If you've got some talent with PhotoShop, the sky's the limit. Really, is it all that important that your travel stories "tell the truth the whole truth and nothing but the truth"? Wouldn't you say that it's much more important to tell an exciting story, with fabulous visuals and lots of interesting details, a story that inspires your friends to get themselves up off the couch and go exploring too? You bet it is!

Game #17

Ridicule
Getting Rid of the Whole Family

I prefer to be true to myself, even at the hazard of incurring the ridicule of others, rather than to be false, and to incur my own abhorrence.
>—Frederick Douglass (1818–1895)
>American abolitionist/statesman

Are you fed up with living in a world full of idiots? Have you had it with inept bosses, lazy employees and lying customers? Do the people in your own household disgust you with their embarrassing habits, their lack of sense and their stupid views? Is it any wonder that you've been doing everything you can to get away from them?

You've played some of the games in this book and may see their value for dealing with jerks. The MOTHER TONGUE Game showed you how this Hell came into your life. The I'M OUTTA HERE Game gave you one way out. And, playing the RE-SPECT Game helps you reevaluate and, subsequently, re-value the people you judge.

Sure, you concede, a person can maintain their own side of the street. But, there's a limit to what you can take before you retaliate. Some people just don't deserve respect, and you've got to strike back. Yet, when you put on those hot pink boxing gloves to play the AIM FOR THE BACK OF THE HEAD Game, are you surprised to see that it's your own face blocking the way to your Big Dream?

Well, it's time to amp up your introspection. As you play these games and as you begin to think and speak differently, it's time to take a closer look at your old attitudes. What part does your judgment play in why these unpleasant people are still in the picture? Are you ready to make a dramatic shift in your perspective as well as in your language patterns, a shift that will once and for all jettison intolerable people from your life?

The truth of the matter is, it's not *who* or *what* you ridicule that causes you sorrow and weariness. It's the fact *that* you ridicule that makes contentment elusive and genuine friendship impossible. For contentment and genuine friendship are grounded in appreciation.

The bad news is, ridicule and appreciation cannot exist simultaneously in the same mind.

The good news is, ridicule and appreciation cannot exist simultaneously in the same mind.

And this means, as you substitute words of appreciation, compassion and esteem, ridicule can no longer keep you in the trance that you live in a world of idiots and fools. This antidote to ridicule works just as well for the entire family of enervating attitudes: sarcasm, criticism, cynicism and mockery.

Step 1. Gratitude. The first attitude you put in place of ridicule is gratitude. In the presence of anyone you feel inclined to ridicule, say "Thank you." It's best to say this out loud, and loudly enough so that the person can hear. However, if you prefer to make this a sub-step, you can say "Thank you" silently at first. This will awaken you to the realization that this person is in your life for a good reason. Saying "Thank you", gives you time to contemplate what that reason is while saving you from saying other words you may later regret. This declaration of gratitude also establishes the possibility of future good will between you.

Step 2. Compassion. Playing a round of the RE-SPECT Game will be a big help before you take this step. Look for whatever attributes you have in common, and be assured, as humans on this planet, you have many more things in common than differences. When you are inclined to speak to or about the person, only give voice to those ideas that will honor, celebrate or bring joy to both the person and your listener.

Step 3. Acceptance. Once you have developed Gratitude and Compassion for this person you used to ridicule, Acceptance is the final step. One of the Webster dictionary's definitions for accept is "to receive willingly," and this is exactly how you respond to this person now. Just as you accept the new day, electricity and fresh air, accept this person as an interesting and worthwhile part of the landscape of your life.

By the time you reach Step 3, you may know the reason why this person is in your life. If not, use this as the focus of a few days of playing the NEW THOT BOX Game. When you do arrive at a reason that make sense to you, take whatever respectful action will enhance that value. You may find that, once you drop your attitude of ridicule, the person simply melts into the background. Now, you can forget his or her imagined shortcomings and redirect your attention toward your own ideals.

Bonus Benefit

Every thought that travels through your mind and every word that comes out of your mouth *first* affects and infects you. Releasing ridicule and the family of related attitudes from the language you use will do much to heal your own self-alienation. As you replace dismissive thoughts and disrespectful words about others with kind regard and genuine interest, you will be amazed at how much more at home you feel with yourself.

Game #18

I Am Not Sorry!
Never Apologize Again

It is a good rule in life never to apologize. The right sort of people do not want apologies, and the wrong sort take a mean advantage of them. —P.G. Wodehouse (1881–1975)
English writer

You never owe anyone an apology. The only debt you owe for past transgressions is forgiveness, namely, forgiveness of your younger self who agreed to participate in condemning you.

Your apology is the evidence that you have agreed to condemn yourself for an earlier decision, a decision made in the now-dead past, which cannot be changed. This, in turn, distances you from your mind that was doing its best when you made the decision. Nevertheless, that same mind is the one on which you must rely for your next decision. And the further you are from harmony with your own mind, the more possible it will be that your next choice will displease both the other person and you.

> **apology** : an admission of error or discourtesy accompanied by an expression of regret; an expression of regret for a mistake or wrong with implied admission of guilt or fault.

Regret, mistake, error, wrong, guilt, fault. These words confirm and sustain a condemning judgment about the past, even though no amount of judgment will ever change what has already happened. The past is over. However, the emotions of fear, shame and humiliation, which are incited by these words, narrow our attention to "fight or flight." In this closed-down state of mind, it's difficult to imagine the next step in the right direction. When we believe these concepts about ourselves and feel these emotions, we are essentially bereft of the resources necessary for making appropriate amends and subsequent wise decisions.

> **sorry**: feeling sorrow, regret, or penitence; inspiring sorrow, pity, scorn, or ridicule.

As you discovered playing the MASTER HYPNOTIST Game, beginning any statement with the words "I am" can cast the speaker instantaneously into a trance of certainty. The person then behaves in unquestioning compliance with the statement. Therefore, to say, "I'm sorry" invokes the "deep distress, sadness and regret" of sorrow. In addition, "sorry" also carries the invitation to others to look upon us with scorn and ridicule.

Hoping to rectify an unacceptable consequence or make effective amends while in a sorrowful, humiliated or apologetic state of mind simply doesn't work. Forcing yourself, or forcing someone else, to apologize is attempting to move toward something that you are naturally inclined to move away from. Being forced toward what repels you only amplifies fear, restricting even further your possible choices for amends.

The social convention of apologizing is prevalent and rarely examined. And, the less we understand the conventions that drive us, the more defensive we are about them and the more hostile we are toward anyone who doesn't go along with them. Nevertheless, as you consider the less-than-useful states that result from this convention, realize how much you can help others, as well as yourself, when you are no longer driven by the habit of apology.

When you apologize to another person in an attempt to reconcile a debt, what you are really doing is playing the *Wake Drives the Boat* Game. In this game, the past is seen as forever creating the future. Those who demand apologies from you are actually admitting that your past behavior is the wake that drives their boat. The demand for your apology is an unwitting attempt to rewrite what happened into something that the "slighted" person can control.

This is a very common and popular game. However, when looked at afresh, do you not see how absurd this is? If yesterday determined today, there would be no new blossoms, no new seasons, no new ideas. We are actually being drawn into an unborn future every day, one that can differ extraordinarily from yesterday. This is so strikingly evident when we look for it.

Yet, regardless of any human will or wish to change it, the past remains the past. And, when your apology cannot give others the control they seek, their resentment, instead of being lessened, is in fact heightened. Very soon, you will commit another "sin" for which another apology will be necessary.

If you are already in an apologetic relationship with someone, notice this. Notice the frequency with which you apologize, how quickly you say "I'm sorry" for little or no reason. You may be so accustomed to using this language pattern that you even begin new conversations with that person by saying, "I'm sorry…." or "Excuse me…."

No amount of apologizing will ever make this better. One or both of you will soon grow weary of this enervating game.

And then, it may seem as though the only way out is to walk away from the relationship. However, that is not so. By dropping apology from your language, you will soon be able to eliminate it from your life. And you do this by playing the I AM NOT SORRY! Game.

Step 1. Begin by consciously noticing other people's responses to what you have said or done. Especially notice the times when other people acknowledge your good work and appreciate what you do.

Step 2. Whenever someone congratulates you, compliments you or expresses appreciation for your contributions, immediately respond with, *"Thank you. I appreciate you and your kind words."* Play the game only in these situations at first. This will awaken you to how good it feels to receive and acknowledge appreciation. This also helps you develop an effective language pattern for keeping your heart open to others. Continue to notice these times and practice the pattern as often as you can for at least a week before moving on to Step 3.

Anyone living his or her own self-guided life does, at times, bump up against other people. The closer we are, the more chances we have to stumble over one another's feet. Playing Steps 3 through 5 is your opportunity to effectively repair a breach or rectify an unintended outcome in your relationships.

Step 3. When someone responds to what you have done or said with anger or criticism, insult or hurt, respond immediately with, *"Thank you. I appreciate you and your valuable feedback."* This response may surprise the other person, so give him or her a few moments. Whether the person welcomes your response or prefers to continue expressing their displeasure, either behavior is fine. As much as you can, listen to their response as legitimate and worthy of a few minutes of your focused attention.

Step 4. Before you respond, give yourself time to decide what you believe is a desirable outcome. For example, you might desire to happily continue a project or an adventure with the person. Maybe you would like to have renewed harmony in the relationship, or you would like to restore respect. Once you know clearly what outcome you would like, insert this outcome in the (X) position in the following suggested texts. (In the examples below, I use the desired outcome of "renewed respect" toward the other person.) A further benefit of taking time before you respond is that the other person will sense your investment in a solution.

Step 5A. When it's time for you to speak, say, *"Thank you. I see/hear/feel/understand now how my decision affected you. Since I can't go back and change the past, what do I need to do now for you to feel respected/(X) ?"* As he or she responds with suggestions, welcome all of the person's ideas. When a suggested idea adequately matches what you can and want to do to make amends, quickly affirm your commitment to doing it. Then, as soon as possible, implement it and move on.

Step 5B. If the person requests an apology, say, *"The issue isn't that the best I could do a moment/a day/a year ago missed the mark. The issue is that I am willing to make amends for the consequence of my actions. So, tell me, what constructive action can I take now for you to know that I really do respect you/(X)?"* As above in Step 5A, listen attentively, eagerly consider the suggestions, and affirm your commitment to do one right away. If none of the suggestions comfortably matches your own ideas, use creative imagination and your sincere desire to repair the situation. Modify one of their ideas into one you are willing to do. Since these ideas are pretty much off the top of the person's head, they will most probably be easily negotiated, if your intentions about satisfying them is clear.

Step 5C. If the person demands an apology, say, *"The question isn't how guilty or ashamed you think I should feel — which is a pretty unresourceful state — the question is, what do I need to do to renew your confidence in my respect for you/(X)?"*

Step 5D. If the person insists that only an apology will do, ask, *"Would you really prefer that I feel guilt or shame rather than being eager to make amends to you?"* Listen with detachment to the answer. Then let the answer guide your decisions about the future of that relationship.

When you decline to apologize, the other person has a couple of choices. She can decide not to stay in your company. Or, she can choose to stay and agree upon amends which will clean the slate on the issue. If you are fortunate, your friend understands the probability that both of you will no doubt make decisions that could result in other unintended consequences in the future. Being accepted for who we are is always the most desirable attitude to share in a relationship.

Your appreciative reply and your willingness to make an acceptable amends, is sure to encourage reasonable people to move forward with you. From anyone who prefers to hold you hostage to shame and blame, and turns away from your offer of amends without apology, you have received an equally valuable gift — freedom from someone else's dungeon. As the person departs, say with all the genuine gratitude you can muster, *"Thank you, I appreciate you and your honesty."*

Bonus Benefit

If you are currently participating in an ongoing apologetic relationship with one person, it's very possible that you're using the same language patterns with other people, too. Continually repeating declarations of being wrong, at fault, guilty or ashamed can thoroughly contaminate your self-perception. As a result, you may come to believe that you must, also, apologize for who you *are*. This is never, ever true. Each human being is as worthy of life as every other human being. Therefore, when it is appropriate for you to address an unintended consequence, offer your amends only for what you said or did, *never* for what you think or who you are. Your mind and your life are your sacred and private domains where no one else deserves to claim authority.

Game #19

Off The Hook
Hanging Out with Your Enemies

*PROSPERO: As you from crimes would pardon'd be,
Let your indulgence set me free.*   *The Tempest*
—William Shakespeare (1564–1616)
English poet/playwright

Do you carry resentments toward others? Are there people you hope you never have to talk to again? Are there others you fear seeing again? Do you find yourself telling stories about people who wronged you, people who deserve to have something bad happen to them? Do you want to get even with someone?

Some years ago, I became aware of how much not being able to forgive was weighing down my life. I felt the presence of a dark, seething place inside me where guilty and (to me) unforgiveable people who had harmed me were still causing me pain. The existence of this blackness that blighted even the brightest moments of my life tormented me. It didn't seem fair that the people who had wronged me could still be doing me damage years later. I came to think of this place as a dungeon.

A common hypnotic trance induction uses the metaphor of going down a winding staircase as a means of going deeper into the subconscious. I was intensely resistant to this visualization because I already feared what was at the bottom of those stairs. However, the torment of being haunted by that place and those awful people finally compelled me to make the journey.

Through self-hypnosis, I traveled down worn stone steps and through dark corridors that ended at a heavy iron door. Behind the door, I could hear muffled cries and sobbing. Then I noticed a skeleton key hanging around my neck. Using the key, I opened the door.

I entered a cold, vast cave. Rusty steel hooks hung head high along the walls. People were suspended from the hooks, hanging by their scapulae and facing outward, their bodies draped against the walls, feet dangling above the floor.

Hidden in the shadows, I peered through the dim light. Here were all my enemies, living and dead. Here was every person against whom I'd ever harbored resentment and nurtured hatred; all the people I'd accused of having hurt, abused or betrayed me, cheated, insulted or lied to me. Impaled, bleeding and decimated, these were the people I'd considered enemies, mortally intent on destroying me. They were crying and moaning. I had heard this sorrowful noise many times before, but had always presumed the sound came from my own suffering self.

As I looked from one forlorn face to the next, I was surprised at feelings of pity and compassion. To keep my hatred burning, I had to look away. But, I'd come here in hopes freeing myself from the torment of this place, and I knew I couldn't keep my eyes averted. It was plain to me then that I had impaled each and every person I had judged as wronging me. I now saw them as *my* prisoners, crying out in pain from the violence *I* was inflicting. They were begging for *my* mercy, not the other way around.

I was the only jailer here. No one else could free any of the hundreds, maybe thousands of people nailed to these walls by my own judgment, fear and hatred. It was clear to me that if I really wanted to be rid of this awful place within myself, I'd have to let them go.

For a time, awareness of the dungeon and its captives was about as far as I got. Yet, I dared to return. Knowing that I was the authority gave me courage. When I went there again, it was with the resolve to release those people I could truly forgive. One by one, I began to take the "criminals" down and set them free, at least the ones I determined had suffered enough. Interestingly, though, as time went on, I discovered that I wanted to release more and more people, even those I would have sworn I'd never "let off the hook."

Playing the OFF THE HOOK Game:
Step 1. Shut your eyes and let yourself relax. Take a few deep breaths. Adjust your body to become as relaxed and comfortable as possible.

Step 2. In your imagination, picture a stairway and begin walking down the steps. As you descend you may begin to hear muffled cries or sobbing. Continue walking down the steps in the direction of those sounds until you find the dungeon door.

Step 3. Open the door with the skeleton key you find hanging around your neck. Let yourself in. Notice the details of the place. It may look like the cave room I described or it may look very different.

Step 4. Realize with complete certainty that you are the only one who can move freely about in this place.

Step 5. Look around at the people hanging there. These are all the people you believed were your enemies, who hated and hurt you, betrayed, abandoned, judged and violated you.

Listen to them sobbing and moaning in pain as they hang from the hooks on the walls.

Step 6. When you are ready, approach a person you wish you never had to be around again. Stare at this person. Regardless of how mean or awful he was to you in the past, he can't hurt you now. If you still hope this person hangs there until doomsday, just know that. That's acceptable for now. Simply open your mind to the possibility that it is your judgment that impaled him. Understand that it is you alone who can ever take him down and let him go.

Step 7. You can leave the dungeon for now, knowing you have discovered the place that houses your grim attachments. Consider, however, that these dark and bloody, sunless dungeon chambers represent the chambers of your own heart. You are the only one who can free the people here because only you have the key. Consider, too, that the "indulgence" by which you set others free, will indeed pardon you of your own "crimes."

Bonus Benefit

During one visit to the dungeon, I became aware of a room I hadn't noticed before, a chamber lined with more weeping and impaled people. However, every person in this room was a younger version of me: toddlers and teenagers, young women and mature women my current age. And there seemed to be as many of these wounded iterations of myself as there were captives in the other room

Staring at these girls and women, I suddenly understood that every time I had impaled someone else, my own anger or resentment had "hooked" me, too. For every person hanging in the first chamber, impaled here was the "me" I had been at that time. Whenever I had condemned someone else for being cruel, I had also condemned myself for being a victim. When I had called someone else a deceiver, I had simultaneously convicted myself for being their fool. For everyone I labeled as heartless, I had punished myself for letting that person hurt me.

I moved closer to look into the faces of these girls and women. I was surprised to see expressions of innocent bewilderment rather than shame, regret or guilt. Then a second insight came to me. I had heard many times that everyone always does their best, given the circumstances and their resources. It now made perfect sense that these girls and women would be bewildered about being impaled. Each one had truly done the best she could at the time.

Amazingly, there were no looks of accusation, hatred or disgust toward me. Instead, each person looked at me with forbearance, compassion and acceptance. They seemed to know that, just as they were suffering in this dungeon, I was suffering, too. I realized, yet again, that only I could set them free. If I hoped to move beyond the sorrows of the past, I would have to take these younger version of myself off the hook, too.

I reached up to unhook a little girl. As soon as I touched her, she fell gently into my arms. When I put her down, she gave me a hug, then ran into the other chamber.

I followed her and watched in amazement as she ran quickly to a little boy who had been "hooked" at the same time for an offense I'd long forgotten. She touched his foot and he stepped easily down. The two of them walked out hand-in-hand, smiling benignly at me where I stood in the shadows.

As they passed by, I felt an enormous weight of old resentment lift from my shoulders. Then I looked where the hooks had been, the ones that had held them on the walls in suffering all those years. Those brutal hooks had turned into white

Easter lilies blooming in the place where each forgiven and liberated person had been.

Step 1. As soon as you can, when you become aware of hurtful, angry or resentful feelings toward anyone, go down into "the dungeon."

Step 2. Instead of going to find the person you thought had wronged you, go deeper into that second room that is reserved for your younger selves. Accept that it is not simply the other person you punish with your judgment, resentment or hatred. Decide now that you have paid enough, been punished enough, suffered enough. Even if that "younger you" was impaled only an hour ago, he or she has truly been here long enough. Go as swiftly and directly as you can to that "other you."

Step 3. Lift yourself off the hook.

Step 4. Stand aside and let this younger self release everyone else who was impaled at the same time.

Step 5. Keep letting them go, these truly innocent younger selves.

Take care, take risks and take no prisoners.

Game #20

Paid In Full!
Rescinding the Price for Your Life and Living Debt-free

For a long time it had seemed to me that life was about to begin — real life. But there was always some obstacle in the way. Something to be got through first, some unfinished business, time still to be served, a debt to be paid. Then life would begin.
—Fr. Alfred D'Souza
Australian author, philosopher

I dearly hope you are, by now, considering that the most important purpose of your life is to enjoy your own company. Does it make sense to you that, once you renew this friendship with your mind, everything else becomes possible? Are you excited to remember that thinking and acting, dreaming and creating, living and being in happy communion with yourself is what you *really need?* The rest — the accolades, the love from others, the stuff — all that is icing on the cake.

However, I understand if someone in your very early years gave you the idea that you, all by yourself, weren't reason enough for your own happiness. The lesson you and I learned in those years was that there was a price on our heads, a debt we owed to the world simply for being alive. And the moment we believed that story was the moment we fell out of Heaven and into the trance that we must pay and pay and pay.

As a hypnotist, I hear many people insist that they have never been hypnotized. And yet, when I ask them if they owe anything to anyone, the answer is invariably yes. For most of us who live in this very wealthy country, the debt is usually financial. And those without money are encumbered with the moral and psychological debts to the society that pays for their meager lodgings and welfare assistance.

The consciousness of debt robs people, not only of their economic well-being, but also of their sense of self-worth. It saps their mental and emotional resources to the point where all they can muster is sufficient productivity to keep the debt in check. Ambition, the courage to develop dreams, and the vitality to reach for new opportunities are dissipated by the worry, fear and exhaustion that accompany debt.

Debt is like ridicule. It's not the amount you actually owe that holds you in chains. It's the belief that you owe someone for your very life that keeps you down and dispirited. It's the way you learned to think and talk about debts. And these include not just monetary obligations, but also the debts one's culture owes to another, the unpaid burdens from past generations, and the debts owed to the past and future. These are the patterns of language and of thought, which you witnessed in childhood and have modeled now for years. These beliefs are the wardens who keep you in debtors' prison.

Once the consciousness of debt infuses a person, it eclipses the courage and daring of imagination, the confidence necessary for invention. When those are gone, where is the hope and desire to do an exemplary job or grow a business with enthusiasm? Even when one's cell expands from a cubicle to a corporate corner office, if the person occupying that office sees the bars of his obligations across the expansive view, he knows he isn't free. The best he can manage is to dully go on about his duties, with the crack of debt's whip ringing in his ears.

Where did these debilitating concepts about debt come from? When so much more has been added to the world by people who boldly act on their vision than those who struggle under their burdens, why is the debt story so popular?

The belief in the burden of debt is the dark side of wanting to belong. Let's look back again to our childhoods. Even though an infant could easily die in a day without the assistance of others, children do not live in debt. Children invest what they have to get what they need. For all of you reading this book, clearly your childhood needs were sufficiently met. And, back then, before you adequately mastered the language and behaviors of your parents or guardians, you did what was necessary to live the full life of a small child, debt-free, from moment to moment.

But as you became more integrated into your family and your culture, as you accepted the story that you needed them and not just the services they provided, you began to believe that belonging was essential to your survival. Once you agreed with that, it was just a matter of time before you accepted everything they believed as true, in order to belong.

But no mother or father would knowingly pass on such a burden to their children if they weren't held by that trance themselves. Not knowing another way of perceiving or believing, each generation takes up the yoke and passes the story of debt on to the next. But why, in an historic time of measureless abundance and open access to every product in the world, are so many people locked into slavery to this consciousness of debt? Why does it pervade collective thought, e.g. at the time of this writing, news about worldwide economic collapse dominates the newspapers, TV talk shows and internet headline services.

So who benefits from your consciousness of debt? The last sentence of the previous paragraph supplies part of the answer. The media profits from reporting the ills of one group and selling that news to another. Keeping you in fear is a sure way to keep you in debt. And, too, corporate creditors profit from your living under this burdensome belief. The trick, of course, is to keep you in debt enough to restrict your impulses to launch into new and possibly less secure directions while not constricting you so tightly that bankruptcy is your only option. Between the media who scares you and the credit card companies who hook you and are now reeling you in at 25% interest, this belief is very profitable for some.

And yet, you cannot hold anyone else in debt when you wish to be free of that prison yourself. This applies as much to those who would keep your attention locked into fearful half-truths and enticed by available credit, as those who raised you in debt.

Invest now in playing the PAID IN FULL! Game and free your mind, as well as your money, to use as you desire.

Step 1. When the thought, *I can't afford it* comes into your mind, play the SAYS WHO? Game.

Step 2. Once you have an answer to SAYS WHO? go into the dungeon of the OFF THE HOOK Game. Go directly into the chamber where your younger selves hang and release that little girl or boy who let herself or himself be convinced that there was a price for life. Once free, that child will go into the other room and release the adult who taught you that belief. Be sure you don't stand in the way! No amount of resentment or anger will bring back a day of your life. And the future you desire cannot come to you as long as you hold these guiltless people in prison.

Step 3. Play the COME HOME! Game. Then, stay seated and continue to breathe calmly and deeply.

Step 4. Shut your eyes. Using your vivid imagination, see yourself doing, having or being the thing you desire. Write or draw this vividly imagined experience on a NEW THOT BOX index card.

Step 5. With the index card from Step 4 in your hands and the vivid image in your mind, play the PLAY WITH YOURSELF Game: As the PRODUCER, determine one particular scene, which happens *after* you acquire what you desire. Then, instruct your WRITER to write a short script, your DIRECTOR to plan the performance, and your ACTOR to rehearse the part.

Step 6. If you're feeling the urge, take a break and USE YOUR DRUGS!

Step 7. For the next seven days, do the following Steps 8-12.

Step 8. Before you go to bed, make sure there's a good supply of index cards and a pen or two on your nightstand.

Step 9. When you lie down in bed, bring your scene from the PLAY WITH YOURSELF Game vividly to mind. As you fall to sleep, experience the scene five times, as follows:

1) Experience it as the Actor at normal speed.

2) Experience it as the Actor in slow motion.

3) Experience it as the Actor in fast motion.

4) Experience it as the Actor with a blindfold on, so you must engage more fully your other senses as you play the scene.

5) Experience it just as you are, pajamas or no pajamas. Notice, when you are the Producer, Writer, Director and Actor, you are perfect in the part, *just as you are*.

Step 10. As you drift into the hypnagogic moment before sleep, repeat to yourself like a lullaby, "It's already paid. It's already paid. It's already paid."

Step 11. As you wake in the morning, sliding back through the hypnopompic moment into this "reality," bring with you whatever thought or idea was last in your dreaming mind. Quickly write that new thought on an index card.

Step 12. Play the I GET TO… Game as often as you can through the week. This will enliven your mind to discover how these new thoughts can turn the scene you are rehearsing into your reality.

Step 13. Drop the word *spend* from your vocabulary. To *spend* literally means, to *use up*, to *exhaust*, to *wear out* and to *squander*. Is it any wonder, then, regardless of what you've "spent" it on, you're exhausted at the end of your workweek, your holiday and even your buying spree?

Wherever you have — up until now — used the word *spend* replace it with the word *invest*. To *invest* means to *furnish with power or authority*, to commit *in order to earn a financial return*, and to *make use of for future benefits*. Keep these definitions in mind whenever you think of using your time or your money. Ask yourself, "What future benefit does this expenditure of my time and/or my money guarantee?" Question, also, the "investments" you make with your attention, your thoughts and your emotions. Decline any invitation that is not an investment in the life you want to live. Period. Turn spending into investing and transform the consciousness of debt into the recognition of your assets and growing wealth.

Bonus Benefit
Don't do me any favors!
… and don't ask me any favors, either.

To do a favor or to accept a favor is to instantly reactivate the state of indebtedness that you have just escaped. Explore all the ways you can pay as you go. Use the NEW THOT BOX Game to discover resources you might not realize you have. Continue to play the I GET TO… Game to keep your mind open to the many choices available. Use the ABOUT FACE! Game to ensure that what you think you want is what you really want. And, remember, you cannot hold anyone else in debt when you wish to be free of that prison yourself.

The next time you would like someone else's help, instead of asking for a favor, first consider what their help is worth to you. Is it $50, or an hour of your own time or talents? Once you determine the value of the favor, offer that up-front in trade for the help you desire. For example, "I'll babysit your children for half a day if you'll edit two chapters of my book." The person can then accept the deal or suggest an alternate barter that more closely meets their desires. If the person says he'll just do the requested work as a favor, thank him and add, "I appreciate your offer, but I've decided to no longer accept favors. I'd much rather make a fair trade right now than obligate myself to an undetermined commitment in the future." The person may take the option of simply giving you what you ask for, which you can then, of course, graciously accept as a *free and clear gift.*

When someone asks you for a favor, let them know that you no longer do favors. Tell them that, when possible, you freely share what you have, and you delight in giving gifts when you can. Otherwise, you are always open to negotiating a trade. Ask the person exactly what she wants and ask her what she thinks it's worth. Upon hearing the value she put on your help, consider if you agree with it. If you don't agree, make a counter offer and negotiate to an agreement that is acceptable to both of you. If you simply don't want to do what she asks, let her know immediately, so she can move on to someone else.

Game #21

Skating Away From the Wall
Authoring Your Life

The promises of this world are, for the most part, vain phantoms; and to confide in one's self, and become something of worth and value is the best and safest course.
— Michelangelo (1475–1564)
Italian sculptor, painter, architect and poet,
considered the creator of the Renaissance

Simply, there is *no mind like your own mind*. As you listen to it for guidance and as you act on its ideas, you will cease to be at war, both inside your head and with the world at large. These games demonstrate that it will always be *your own mind* that decides and determines what your life will be. It will always be *your own voice* that dictates who you are.

With every word you speak, you are writing, today, the life you will live tomorrow. Are you feeling the excitement of this possibility right now? Have you posted the sign "Author at Work" on your door to inspire yourself? Are you eager to unplug the media, tune out the opinions of others and tune in to that spectacular mind inside your own head?

Whatever your age, you've spent enough time being skeptical about your own worth. Free yourself from the illusion that the world "out there" is more responsible for your life than you are. If you really intend to live beyond the battle with a mind "that won't shut the @#&* up!," now is the time to accept the authorship of the rest of your life.

Play the SKATING AWAY FROM THE WALL Game. Develop increasing reliance on your own mind, appreciate your own thoughts, and glide out into the center of your own life.

Step 1. On a NEW THOT BOX index card, write *I AM THE AUTHOR OF MY LIFE*. Keep this card with you for the next week.

Step 2. Whenever you hear yourself use the phrases of the MASTER HYPNOTIST Game, *"I am," "I know," "I think,"* or *"I believe,"* take out this card and read it. Take a few moments to ask and answer the question, "Did the statement I just made tell the story I want to author?" If the answer is no, do an instant replay in your mind. Restate what you said in such a way that it does tell your chosen story.

Step 3. Pick a time of day when you are among other people. Have a stack of index cards handy. For the next week, commit to listening to *your* contributions to the conversation. How many of your ideas are new, stimulating and constructive? When you are aware of a new thought, write it on a card. Later, add the card to your NEW THOT BOX.

Step 4. Notice how often what you say simply repeats or paraphrases what you heard someone else say. Whether the statements you make are about you or about the world, every word out of your mouth weaves indelibly into the story of your life. Pay attention to how much of your life you author and how much is authored by Fox News, the Wall Street Journal, dismissive gossip or anonymous bloggers.

Step 5. Select your favorite public person — an athlete, political leader, entertainer, writer, musician. On a sheet of paper, write ten qualities you admire or adore about this person.

Notice what you feel as you do this — admiration, interest, eagerness. Maybe you also feel envy or jealousy.

Step 6. Turn the paper over and write ten qualities you admire or adore about yourself. Notice what you feel now. Are you as eager? Do you feel as much admiration? If you don't feel as enthusiastic right now, can you imagine how wonderful it is when you do feel as much or more eagerness to write about your own life as about someone else's? As you continue to play these games and as you re-friend your mind, these marvelous feelings are sure to embrace you.

Step 7. Repeat Step 3. of the I'M OUTTA HERE! Game. This time, turn off and set aside all media devices, newspapers, books and music for an hour. Devote a full hour to listening to your own mind. If you can, go outside; your mind will feel at home there. Take a pen and a few index cards. Honor whatever new thoughts come, and write them down.

Step 8. Every day, during this hour, make a new list of another ten qualities or attributes you admire or adore about yourself. By the end of just one week, you will have authored the first chapter of the book about the one person who truly deserves to be your hero.

Step 9. Notice any tension or amplified stress you feel. Maybe it's enough to incline you to USE YOUR DRUGS! Go ahead. Be compassionate with yourself.

Step 10. Keep skating away from old dependencies on what other people think and what other people have written. Author your own truths, and act on them as often as you can.

Bonus Benefit

Get a box that will hold a ream of standard paper. Select seven photographs of yourself taken from when you were ten to your present age. Every day for the next week, consider one picture a day and, on a sheet of paper write ten things you admire or adore about yourself in the photo. Staple the paper to the picture and put into the box.

Add the lists you wrote in Step 8. These are the beginnings of your autobiography!

Section Three

**** Bonus Game ****

Wherever you are in life, if you're still breathing, there's always a yonder, a new day, another door to walk through and another adventure to enjoy. And, each one of these opportunities begins with an awakening in your mind. May you play on with an eager and happy heart, far beyond the games in this book. And may you enjoy every new thought and every new choice as an added bonus to your own magnificent life.

Game #22

Who / What
... are you saving it for?

If you deliberately plan on being less than you are capable of being, then I warn you that you'll be unhappy for the rest of your life. —Abraham Maslow (1908–1970)
American psychologist

We've come to the end of the book, Dear Reader. May this coincide with a great new chapter in your life. Although I can't know what you've gained from playing these games, I certainly hope that you are now enjoying a sense of reconnection with your own fine mind. I imagine that you now recognize the value of serving your own great ideas and are experiencing a fine friendship with your mind when you do.

In order to keep your eyes on the prize, play the WHO/WHAT Game whenever you hesitate to step boldly into your next Big Dream.

Step 1. On half a dozen index cards, write in great big letters in the center of the cards, "WHO..."

Step 2. On the reverse side, in the same place and with the same size letters, write "WHAT..."

Step 3. In small letters along the bottom of both sides of the card, write "...are you saving it for?"

Step 4. Distribute the cards around your house and office, in your car and in the pockets of your favorite coat.

Step 5. Whenever you hesitate to take another step closer to your Big Dream, take out one of these cards. Invest the next 60 seconds playing the COME HOME! Game. Then ask yourself the questions on the card, allowing them to encourage you onward, to keep moving toward your own intentions, your own chosen destinations

Step 6. However, if you do come up with an answer that you consider acceptable, write it on the card. Commit to incorporating that person or thing into your plans as soon as you can. Then, swiftly resume the exciting adventure of writing your own fantastic life across the sky.

Index

Symbols
@#&*, 18, 51, 54, 62, 109

A
acceptance, 85, 98
addiction, 43, 44, 46, 47
adjectives, 54, 55
Ali, Muhammad, 48, 52
antidote, 53, 84
antithesis, 60
apologies, 87, 89
apologize, 87-89, 92, 93
apology, 87, 89, 90-92
appreciate, 54, 90, 92, 106, 109
appreciation, 63, 84, 90
attention, 7, 25-28, 30-33, 51, 61, 62, 64, 67, 70, 71, 85, 88, 90, 103, 105, 109
awaken, 30-32, 35, 37, 39, 84, 90

B
Bacon, Sir Francis, 74
behavior, 15, 43-45, 66, 89, 90, 102
belief,
Bennett, Robert F., 34
big dream, 48-52, 61, 65, 81, 84, 113, 114
blame, 92
boxing gloves, 49, 51, 84
breathe, 19, 20, 104
Buck, Pearl S., 40

C
Carnegie, Dale, 58
childhood, 11, 66, 101, 102
children, 12, 66, 102, 106
choice, 32, 34, 35, 38, 45, 46, 68, 80, 81, 87, 88, 92, 106, 112
communion, 12, 100
comparison, 37
compassion, 15, 71, 84, 85, 95, 98, 110
condemnation, 47, 70, 72
consciousness, 101-103, 105
control, 18, 31, 33, 34, 62, 66, 89
courage, 35, 58, 65, 96, 101
creative, 23, 37, 70, 82, 91
crimes, 94, 97
curious, 31, 46, 73, 81

D
D'Souza, Fr. Alfred, 100
debt, 12, 13, 33, 87, 89, 100-103, 105, 106
demand, 77, 89, 92
detachment, 47, 92
director, 75-77, 104
discovery, 15, 37
distractions, 25, 63
Douglass, Frederick, 83
drugs, 43, 44, 46, 47, 104, 110

E
Easter lilies, 99

effortless, 20, 22, 42, 50
Ehrmann, Max, 18
Einstein, Albert, 36
enchantment,
encouragement, 7, 35
enemy, 12, 49

F

fear, 11, 21, 23, 58-60, 62, 66, 67, 88, 94-96, 101, 103
freedom, 32, 34, 92
fulfillment, 49, 50

G

Goddard, Neville, 30

H

happiness, 11, 12, 17, 28, 34, 53, 100
heaven, 54-57, 59, 101
hell, 17, 54-57, 59, 83
Hierarchy of Needs, 60, 63
home, 5, 18, 19, 20, 21, 45, 46, 50, 57, 58, 72, 77, 80, 86, 104, 110, 114
house manager, 75, 76
hypnagogic, 50, 62, 75, 104
hypnopompic, 105
hypnotic, 27, 30, 31, 60, 94
hypnotist, 27, 28, 30, 33, 34, 36, 45, 46, 88, 101, 109

I

imagination, 12, 23, 30-34, 36, 39, 48-50, 62, 72, 75, 82, 91, 96, 101, 104
impossible, 40, 84
index cards, 37, 50, 51, 57, 62, 63, 67, 72, 77, 104, 105, 109, 110, 113
indifference, 47
individual, 45, 75
indulgence, 94, 97
influence, 16, 26, 36, 37, 39, 45, 46, 62
insight, 36, 98

intelligence, 36
intention, 17, 36, 46, 50, 62-64, 72, 81, 91, 114
invest, 12, 25, 26, 46, 50, 60, 64, 80, 81, 102, 103, 105, 114
investment, 26, 91, 105

J

James, William, 11
judgment, 45, 47, 70-72, 84, 88, 96, 97, 99

K

Karrass, Dr. Chester L., 79

L

language, 35, 40, 54, 55, 65, 84, 86, 89, 90, 93, 101, 102
lullaby, 104
Lunacy Cycle, 15

M

Maltz, Maxwell, 27
Maslow, Abraham 60, 66, 113
metaphor, 94
Michelangelo, 108
mile-high club, 82

N

New Zealand, 79

O

observations, 40, 41, 72
off the hook, 94, 96, 98, 99, 103
opinions, 19, 25, 28, 36, 49, 51, 108

P

pardon, 94, 97
peace, 5, 16, 18, 58-60
perception, 41, 42, 55, 66, 68, 93
Polo, Marco, 82
possibilities, 11, 15, 42, 64, 67

power, 30, 34, 36, 105
prisoners, 95, 99
producer, 74-77, 104
promises, 62, 108
purgatory, 54-56, 77
purpose, 12, 22, 31, 59, 63, 72, 100

R

re-friend, 13, 39, 110
re-spect, 70-73, 83, 85
refresh, 19, 20, 22, 32
regret, 15, 85, 87, 88, 98
relaxation, 18, 21, 22, 30, 31, 59, 62
relief, 17, 18, 41, 44, 45, 53
resentment, 89, 94, 95, 97-99, 103
ridicule, 71, 83-86, 88, 101

S

sadness, 44, 88
scared s**tless club, 58-60, 62
screensaver, 21, 22
self-actualization, 61
self-alienation, 86
self-discovery, 15, 37
self-hypnosis, 95
Seneca, 21
Shakespeare, William, 94
shame, 88, 92, 98

sin, 89
sleep, 12, 44, 50, 75, 104
sorrow, 84, 88, 98
sorry, 87-90
star, 75, 76
story, 29, 35, 47, 60, 73, 82, 101, 102, 109
stress, 44, 45, 110
suffering, 95, 98
suggestion, 27, 28, 31, 60, 66, 81, 91
surrender, 44, 45
survival, 59, 102

T

take no prisoners, 99
tension, 17, 22, 23, 44, 45, 110
trance, 27, 28, 30-34, 44, 46, 53, 57, 62-64, 80, 84, 88, 94, 101, 102
Twain, Mark 54, 65

U

unconscious, 34
unhappiness, 12

W

Wodehouse, P. G., 87
worry, 13, 21, 23, 101
writer, 75, 77, 104, 109

If you enjoyed this book and would like to pass a copy on to someone else, please check with your local bookstore, favorite online bookseller, or order directly from the publisher:

Prime Number Press
Post Office Box 898
Sausalito, CA 94966
www.primenumberpress.com

Additional titles in the *Games for Your Mind* Series:

The Greatest Story Ever Told... Is Yours:
21 Games for Re-Discovering and Staying Yourself in a World of Change (Prime Number Press: 2010)

Don't Do As I Do!
21 Games for Teens Who Want to Bypass Their Parents' Mistakes
(Prime Number Press: 2011)

Befriending Yourself Before You Die
21 Games for Elders Whose Children have given Them Up for Dead
(Prime Number Press: 2011)

Thanks Mom & Dad
21 Games for Redefining Yourself and Your Life
(Prime Number Press: 2012)

Arms Wide Open!
21 Games for the Truly Adventurous
(Prime Number Press: 2012)

For updates and information about the *Games for Your Mind* Series, plus other nonfiction and fiction books, eBooks, scripts, audio and video products and New Thots by A.T. Lynne, please visit the author's website: www.atlynne.com

www.ingramcontent.com/pod-product-compliance
Lightning Source LLC
Chambersburg PA
CBHW031255290426
44109CB00012B/595